COMMUNICATING SOCIAL SCIENCE RESEARCH TO POLICYMAKERS

APPLIED SOCIAL RESEARCH METHODS SERIES

1. **SURVEY RESEARCH METHODS (Second Edition)**
   by FLOYD J. FOWLER, Jr.
2. **INTEGRATING RESEARCH (Second Edition)**
   by HARRIS M. COOPER
3. **METHODS FOR POLICY RESEARCH**
   by ANN MAJCHRZAK
4. **SECONDARY RESEARCH (Second Edition)**
   by DAVID W. STEWART
   and MICHAEL A. KAMINS
5. **CASE STUDY RESEARCH (Second Edition)**
   by ROBERT K. YIN
6. **META-ANALYTIC PROCEDURES FOR SOCIAL RESEARCH (Revised Edition)**
   by ROBERT ROSENTHAL
7. **TELEPHONE SURVEY METHODS (Second Edition)**
   by PAUL J. LAVRAKAS
8. **DIAGNOSING ORGANIZATIONS (Second Edition)**
   by MICHAEL I. HARRISON
9. **GROUP TECHNIQUES FOR IDEA BUILDING (Second Edition)**
   by CARL M. MOORE
10. **NEED ANALYSIS**
    by JACK McKILLIP
11. **LINKING AUDITING AND METAEVALUATION**
    by THOMAS A. SCHWANDT
    and EDWARD S. HALPERN
12. **ETHICS AND VALUES IN APPLIED SOCIAL RESEARCH**
    by ALLAN J. KIMMEL
13. **ON TIME AND METHOD**
    by JANICE R. KELLY
    and JOSEPH E. McGRATH
14. **RESEARCH IN HEALTH CARE SETTINGS**
    by KATHLEEN E. GRADY
    and BARBARA STRUDLER WALLSTON
15. **PARTICIPANT OBSERVATION**
    by DANNY L. JORGENSEN
16. **INTERPRETIVE INTERACTIONISM**
    by NORMAN K. DENZIN
17. **ETHNOGRAPHY (Second Edition)**
    by DAVID M. FETTERMAN
18. **STANDARDIZED SURVEY INTERVIEWING**
    by FLOYD J. FOWLER, Jr.
    and THOMAS W. MANGIONE
19. **PRODUCTIVITY MEASUREMENT**
    by ROBERT O. BRINKERHOFF
    and DENNIS E. DRESSLER
20. **FOCUS GROUPS**
    by DAVID W. STEWART
    and PREM N. SHAMDASANI
21. **PRACTICAL SAMPLING**
    by GARY T. HENRY
22. **DECISION RESEARCH**
    by JOHN S. CARROLL
    and ERIC J. JOHNSON
23. **RESEARCH WITH HISPANIC POPULATIONS**
    by GERARDO MARIN
    and BARBARA VANOSS MARIN
24. **INTERNAL EVALUATION**
    by ARNOLD J. LOVE
25. **COMPUTER SIMULATION APPLICATIONS**
    by MARCIA LYNN WHICKER
    and LEE SIGELMAN
26. **SCALE DEVELOPMENT**
    by ROBERT F. DeVELLIS
27. **STUDYING FAMILIES**
    by ANNE P. COPELAND
    and KATHLEEN M. WHITE
28. **EVENT HISTORY ANALYSIS**
    by KAZUO YAMAGUCHI
29. **RESEARCH IN EDUCATIONAL SETTINGS**
    by GEOFFREY MARUYAMA
    and STANLEY DENO
30. **RESEARCHING PERSONS WITH MENTAL ILLNESS**
    by ROSALIND J. DWORKIN
31. **PLANNING ETHICALLY RESPONSIBLE RESEARCH**
    by JOAN E. SIEBER
32. **APPLIED RESEARCH DESIGN**
    by TERRY E. HEDRICK,
    LEONARD BICKMAN,
    and DEBRA J. ROG
33. **DOING URBAN RESEARCH**
    by GREGORY D. ANDRANOVICH
    and GERRY RIPOSA
34. **APPLICATIONS OF CASE STUDY RESEARCH**
    by ROBERT K. YIN
35. **INTRODUCTION TO FACET THEORY**
    by SAMUEL SHYE
    and DOV ELIZUR
    with MICHAEL HOFFMAN
36. **GRAPHING DATA**
    by GARY T. HENRY
37. **RESEARCH METHODS IN SPECIAL EDUCATION**
    by DONNA M. MERTENS
    and JOHN A. McLAUGHLIN
38. **IMPROVING SURVEY QUESTIONS**
    by FLOYD J. FOWLER, Jr.
39. **DATA COLLECTION AND MANAGEMENT**
    by MAGDA STOUTHAMER-LOEBER
    and WELMOET BOK VAN KAMMEN
40. **MAIL SURVEYS**
    by THOMAS W. MANGIONE
41. **QUALITATIVE RESEARCH DESIGN**
    by JOSEPH A. MAXWELL
42. **ANALYZING COSTS, PROCEDURES, PROCESSES, AND OUTCOMES IN HUMAN SERVICES**
    by BRIAN T. YATES
43. **DOING LEGAL RESEARCH**
    by ROBERT A. MORRIS, BRUCE D. SALES,
    and DANIEL W. SHUMAN
44. **RANDOMIZED EXPERIMENTS FOR PLANNING AND EVALUATION**
    by ROBERT F. BORUCH
45. **MEASURING COMMUNITY INDICATORS**
    by PAUL J. GRUENEWALD,
    ANDREW J. TRENO, GAIL TAFF,
    and MICHAEL KLITZNER
46. **MIXED METHODOLOGY**
    by ABBAS TASHAKKORI and
    CHARLES TEDDLIE
47. **NARRATIVE RESEARCH**
    by AMIA LIEBLICH, RIVKA TUVAL-
    MASHIACH, and TAMAR ZILBER
48. **COMMUNICATING SOCIAL SCIENCE RESEARCH TO POLICYMAKERS**
    by ROGER VAUGHAN and
    TERRY F. BUSS

COMMUNICATING SOCIAL SCIENCE RESEARCH TO POLICYMAKERS

Roger J. Vaughan
Terry F. Buss

Applied Social Research Methods Series
Volume 48

SAGE Publications
International Educational and Professional Publisher
Thousand Oaks London New Delhi

For information:

SAGE Publications, Inc.
2455 Teller Road
Thousand Oaks, California 91320
E-mail: order@sagepub.com

SAGE Publications Ltd.
6 Bonhill Street
London EC2A 4PU
United Kingdom

SAGE Publications India Pvt. Ltd.
M-32 Market
Greater Kailash I
New Delhi 110 048 India

Printed in the United States of America

Library of Congress Cataloging-in-Publication Data

Vaughan, Roger J.
  Communicating social science research to policymakers /
by Roger J. Vaughan & Terry F. Buss.
      p. cm.—(Applied social research methods; v. 48)
  Includes bibliographical references and index.
  ISBN 0-8039-7215-6 (cloth: alk. paper)
  ISBN 0-8039-7216-4 (pbk.: alk. paper)
    1. Social sciences—Research. 2. Communication in the social sciences.
3. Social policy. I. Buss, Terry F. II. Title.
III. Series: Applied social research methods series; v. 48.
H62 .V35 1998
300'.7'2—ddc21   98-40061

This book is printed on acid-free paper.

98 99 00 01 02 03 04 7 6 5 4 3 2 1

Acquiring Editor:	C. Deborah Laughton
Editorial Assistant:	Eileen Carr
Production Editor:	Sanford Robinson
Editorial Assistant:	Nevair Kabakian
Typesetter:	Lynn Miyata

Contents

Preface   ix

Acknowledgments   xiii

1. Offering Advice   1
   Rule 1: Know the Limits of Social Science   2
   Rule 2: Be Practical   5
   Cost-Benefit Analysis and Policy Analysis   6
   Policy Analysis and Medicine Compared   7
   Summary   13

2. Assessing   14
   Rule 1: Maintain an Open Mind   15
   Rule 2: Look Behind the Numbers   19
   Rule 3: Learn the History of the Issue   25
   Summary   27
   Case Studies   27

3. Diagnosing   30
   Rule 1: Develop Competing Hypotheses   32
   Rule 2: Determine Whether the Problem
      Is Caused by Private Actions   33
   Systemic Problems Arising From Private Actions   34
   Nonsystemic Problems Arising From Private Actions   36
   Rule 3: Determine Whether the Problem Is
      Caused by Government Intervention   38
   Systemic Problems Resulting From Public Actions   38
   Nonsystemic Problems Resulting From Public Actions   39
   Rule 4: Analyze Hypotheses   40
   Rule 5: Follow Up on the Diagnosis   41
   Summary   42
   Case Study   42

4. Prescribing   **45**
Rule 1: Select the Appropriate Baseline for
    Decision Making   48
Rule 2: Assign Priorities   50
Rule 3: Weigh Relative Risks   51
Rule 4: Create a Diversified Policy Portfolio   52
Rule 5: Define Options Clearly   52
Rule 6: Examine Today's Actions Against
    Tomorrow's Options   53
Rule 7: Know the Policy Timetable   54
Rule 8: Know the Players   56
Rule 9: Know the Policy Vocabulary   57
Rule 10: Consider Placebos   58
Rule 11: Measure Options in Terms of
    Opportunities   58
Rule 12. Avoid Common Pitfalls   59
Rule 13: Compare Options   64
Net Present Value   65
Internal Rate of Return   65
Discounting the Future   65
Discounting for Risk   66
Rule 14: Focus on Outcomes, Not Process   66
Rule 15: Consider Starting Over   67
Rule 16: Know When to Give Up   67
Rule 17: Develop a Communications Strategy
    for the Policy   68
Summary   69
Case Studies   70
Case Study 1. Youth Unemployment   70
Case Study 2. Building a Highway Link   72

5. Prognosticating   **75**
Why Forecast?   76
Who Should Forecast?   78
*What Forecasting Techniques Are Available
    and Work Best?*   79
Judgment   81
How Accurate Are Forecasts?   84
Rule 1: Garbage In Yields Garbage Out   85
Rule 2: Use Multiple Techniques to Forecast,
    Then Look for Convergence   85

Rule 3: When Forecasts Diverge, Consider
    Averaging Them   86
Rule 4: Look for Turning Points   87
Rule 5: Monitor Forecasts Using Prospective
    Data   88
Summary   88
Case Study   89

6. **Evaluating**   **92**
    Rule 1: Measure Program Performance   93
    Rule 2: State Program Goals Clearly   95
    Rule 3: Develop Yardsticks for Measuring
        Progress   96
    Rule 4: Create Incentives for Good Performance   98
    Rule 5: Anticipate Opposition   99
    Rule 6: Evaluate the Evaluators   103
    Summary   104
    Case Studies   104
        *Case 1. Measuring Policy Outcomes in Oregon and
            Minnesota*   104
        Case 2. Florida's Policy Accountability System 105

7. **Figuring Out What to Say**   **107**
    Rule 1: Analyze Policy, Not Politics   108
    Rule 2: Keep It Simple   109
    Rule 3: Communicate Reasoning as Well as
        Bottom Lines   112
    Rule 4: Use Numbers Sparingly   114
    Rule 5: Elucidate, Don't Advocate   115
    Rule 6: Identify Winners and Losers   116
    Rule 7: Don't Overlook Unintended
        Consequences   118
    Summary   121

8. **Deciding How to Say It**   **122**
    Rule 1: Write to Think   124
    Rule 2: Don't Fear First Drafts   124
    Rule 3: Show, Don't Tell   127
    Rule 4: Be Brief and Clear   131
    Rule 5: Build the Story With Paragraphs   133
    Rule 6: Write Clear Sentences   135

Rule 7: Omit Needless Words   138
Rule 8: Avoid Jargon   140
Afterword   143
Summary   143

References   **144**

Index   **151**

About the Authors   **159**

Preface

EXPERTS GONE WRONG

About forty years ago, certain persons went to Laputa; and after about five months continuance came back with a very little smattering in mathematicks, but full of the volatile spirits acquired in that airy region. These persons upon their return begun to dislike the management of all things below; and fell into schemes of putting all arts, sciences, languages, and mechanicks upon a new foot. To this end they procured a royal patent for erecting an Academy of Projectors in Lagado; and the humour prevailed so strongly among the people that there is not a town of any consequence in the kingdom without such an academy. In these colleges, the professors contrive new rules and methods of agriculture and building, and new instruments and tools of all trades and manufactures, whereby, as they undertake, one man shall do the work of ten; a palace may be built in a week, of materials so durable that they last forever without repairing. All the fruits of the earth shall come to maturity at whatever season we think fit to chuse, and increase an hundred fold more than they do at present; with innumerable other happy proposals. The only inconvenience is that none of these projects are yet brought to perfection; and in the mean time, the whole country lies in waste, the houses in ruins, and the people without food or cloathes. By all of which, instead of being discouraged, they are fifty times more violently bent upon prosecuting their schemes, driven equally on by hope and despair.

—Jonathan Swift, *Gulliver's Travels* (1711)

Our book's dual purpose is to (a) help professors and students better understand the "real world" of public policy and effectively communicate with practitioners who make and execute it, and (b) help practitioners think more systematically about what they do in the policy arena, introspection they seldom have time for, except perhaps in memoirs published after retirement or leaving office. Our hope is that by bringing producers and consumers of policy analysis together, policy making and policy implementation will improve (see also, Hamilton, 1992; Majchrzak, 1984). At present, the gap between policy analysts in academe and decision makers and analysts in government is wide, perhaps widening (Kaufman, 1995; Whiteman, 1986), and should be closed for the benefit of both (Goldhamer, 1978).

We've organized our book around *rules of thumb* (see Safire, 1998, for an interesting discussion of this concept) and *cases*, peppered with examples we think represent good practice—we hope, best practice—in the art of policy analysis. These rules are not etched in stone, inviolable, exhaustive, or even mutually exclusive. Indeed, policy analysts and decision makers may violate one or more, perhaps all on occasion, in the interest of their art and political exigency. The rules represent considerations policy analysts should think about before releasing their work to decision makers. Likewise, decision makers should run down the list of rules in evaluating policy work presented to them by experts. The bottom line, though, should always be: Do what works best.

The examples and cases offered in our book were drawn from actual, often heated, controversial, sometimes ambiguous, and frequently recurring policy issues. Some readers might disagree with our interpretations. Our purpose is not to argue the merits of any particular case but to encourage policy analysts and decision makers to think more critically not only about their own views but also about the views of others. Good policy analysis arises out of the clash of disparate, contradictory, conflicting ideas, rather than from preconceived theories or ideological visions of the world. Theory and ideology may win out on selected issues in the end, but only after careful evaluation according to rules of the art laid out here.

Policy analysis can be mysterious to most people, even those who teach or study it, because it is something few actually experience in practice. It is often well hidden from outsiders. Policy analysis occurs off stage, sometimes in camera even in academe, whereas politicians soak up the limelight. Many public policy textbooks offer what the authors would like to see policy analysts and decision makers do, often in ways that are unhelpful or unrealistic. Or textbook authors represent policy without really knowing how the system works. We've tried to make the policy process more real by linking it to another professional activity that most people understand and have direct experience with—being a physician's patient. The process physicians follow in assessing, diagnosing, treating, and monitoring patients is uncannily the same as that of policy analysts. Other professions—auto mechanics, airline pilots, photocopy repair technicians, or software troubleshooters—might have served as well. Theirs is a world of checklists for decision making that apply most but not all of the time. Throughout the book, we connect medical and policy models to help make sense of the latter.

This book is a practical guide written primarily for policy analysts in academe who either would like to have their ideas considered by public decision makers or who want to train their students in skills necessary to survive and thrive in the policy arena—whether as experts or decision makers themselves. We eschew any discussion of theory or explanation, and we offer nothing to advance social scientific method, statistical applications, or data processing techniques. This knowledge is amply covered elsewhere and is assumed to be the stock and trade of solid academic training (e.g., Clower, 1995; DeHaven-Smith, 1988; Feyerabend, 1993; MacRae & Whittington, 1997; Ripley, 1985; Weimer & Vining, 1992, to name a few). Instead, we're interested in helping those who have academic training or are about to acquire it work effectively in the policy arena, rather than against or outside it as part of their own separate community of scholars (Frey & Eichenberger, 1993; Goldhamer, 1978; Kaufman, 1995; McCloskey, 1985b; Stigler, 1984).

Mainstream social science policy analysis is an important source, at least potentially, of information for policy analysts and decision makers, but it is not the only source, nor is it necessarily the best source. Policy analysts in government must examine a wide variety of competing information, not just that conforming to the canons of social science research methods, in developing alternatives for decision makers. "Nonscientific" yet credible information often provides insight into policy missing in social science reports. Journalists, advocacy groups, think tanks, unions, political parties, associations, and bureaucracies all know how to provide decision makers and their experts with information in a form they need. Indeed, their livelihoods depend on it. Social scientists must learn to compete.

Social science research has well-known limitations that keep it from being taken seriously by decision makers. Research is often too irrelevant, impractical, theoretical, technical, and inaccessible to be of interest to practitioners (Frey & Eichenberger, 1993; Hamilton, 1992; Kaufman, 1995). On the one hand, scholars respecting scientific method and professional norms refuse to draw out the policy implications of their work. As a consequence, others not so restricted will draw portions of it out of context and use it anyway, sometimes inappropriately, or, worse, ignore it all together. On the other hand, scholars exploiting their status as objective social scientists in prestigious universities offer policy prescriptions to decision makers that are no more than rank speculation; bald advocacy without foundation; or, in the words of one observer, expressions of sheer "hope." Decision makers do not want information billed as objective, mainstream, or consensual when it is not (Hamilton, 1992). Somewhere in between these two extremes lies the market for social science policy analysis: information that is scientifically valid, yet packaged for decision makers.

In places, we are critical of social science research, not because we devalue it—indeed, both of us have sacrificed thousands of trees writing professional journal articles for academe. Rather, we believe that for the discipline to be of use to decision makers it must change or at least accommodate practitioners. Social scientists are too enamored with and arrogant about their methods in ways that are often unjustified and certainly unacceptable to practitioners (Kaufman, 1995). This book may not convince some academics to change, but we hope that it will help those desiring to step out of their traditional roles and participate effectively in policy debates (see also, Frey & Eichenberger, 1993).

We address policy issues from all three levels of government, including quasi-governmental organizations and not-for-profits, which have become an integral part of the policy process. The rules laid out below are intended to apply to policy generally, regardless of the context. This in itself is unusual: Most policy textbooks are biased toward federal policy and national agencies.

We use the term *decision maker* rather than *policymaker* throughout the book. For us, policymakers are a subset of decision makers. This is intentional. Too often policy analysis focuses on policymakers to the exclusion of high-level officials who do not make policy but affect it in innumerable ways through administration, especially implementation and evaluation. So, we concern ourselves not only with presidents, governors, and mayors, but also with legislative leadership, agency or organization heads, political leaders, and of course their staffs.

Now, on to the rules.

Acknowledgments

Many people helped us prepare this book. The Ohio Board of Regents, under its Urban University Program, provided a grant to develop a guide to writing policy papers for policy analysis and public decision makers. Robert Pollard, senior economist with the U.S. General Accounting Office, reviewed and commented on successive manuscript drafts. Jacques Bagur, economic consultant from Baton Rouge, Louisiana; the late Jack Brizius of the Pennsylvania-based policy consulting firm of Brizius and Foster; Edward W. Hill, professor of Urban Studies, Cleveland State University; William Nothdurft, policy consultant from Bethesda, Maryland; commentator David Osborne, author of *Reinventing Government;* and Mark Popovich, policy analyst with the National Academy of Public Administration (NAPA); and Barbara Dyer, also at NAPA, carefully criticized earlier drafts.

We also thank policymakers and experts in state and local governments who shared insights into their craft, and, of course, student and practitioner participants in numerous policy seminars helped immeasurably in idea development. We used earlier drafts of this manuscript to train high-ranking public officials in Eastern Europe, Russia, and South Africa under grants from the U.S. Information Agency: Hungarian members of Parliament, 20 mayors, and city finance directors; Romanian physicians seeking public health degrees; Russian oblast ministers in seven regions/cities (Nizhny Novgorod, Saratov, Urals Region, Siberia, Far East, Vladimir, and Moscow); and South African provincial public finance directors appointed by newly elected President Nelson Mandela. Although we have not included foreign case study materials here, we benefited greatly by trying to explain the American policy process to those with little knowledge of it.

Giving us generous assistance does not make anyone else responsible for errors and clumsy writing.

To Anna and Laura

1

Offering Advice

Public decision makers need expert advice. For their part, experts desire, in the words of the late Aaron Wildavsky, "to speak truth to power" (Wildavsky, 1979). Despite a mutual interest in communication, commerce in policy ideas and information between academic experts and decision makers is meager. Differences in language, time horizons, perceptions of importance, values, perceived roles and responsibilities, and methods separate the two (Hamilton, 1992; Kaufman, 1995). Experts care about how the world works in general; decision makers about how specific bits of it might work tomorrow (Behn, 1981). Experts adhere to scientific methods intended to ensure knowledge acquisition in an orderly, rigorous, and replicable manner; decision makers must decide without luxury of proving themselves correct. Experts debate ideas among themselves; decision makers must decide in an unforgiving public glare. Warren G. Nutter, a professor who became Assistant Secretary of Defense, is reputed to have said, "In the academic world you think now and decide never; and in government it's exactly the other way round." Stephen Toulmin (1958) was fond of saying that less evidence was required to sentence a person to death than to confirm a theory through empirical research.

Because they look at things differently, academics and practitioners are suspicious of one other (Goldhamer, 1978; Sabatier, 1978). Academics suppose politicians bend truth to win votes and amass power. For many academics, practitioners can be unscrupulous opportunists. Political behavior since Watergate has done little to dispel this belief. For example, in a survey conducted by the Advancement of Sound Science Coalition, researchers found that 83% of physicians and scientists involved in environmental health believed that government officials misuse science to support predetermined, dubious, unsupported policies for asbestos, smoking, dioxins, and pesticides. Sixty-eight percent reported being under great pressure to produce politically correct results. And 82% believe that the public does not understand environmental policy because it is not properly explained by policymakers ("Junk Science," 1994). Practitioners suspect that academics avoid definitive conclusions to escape professional criticism,

1

to market research, to gain promotion, or to get published. For many practitioners, academics appear wishy-washy, self-interested, and irrelevant. Many are perceived to be no different from the politicians they disdain when using faulty research to further ideological or political ends. Misperception discourages cooperation. But the gap can be bridged (Kaufman, 1995; Sy, 1987).

The time to bridge the gap is now. Academics face declining research budgets, increased competition from other researchers, reduced resources, and sometimes decreasing access to decision makers, while at the same time coming under pressure to bring in grant and contract moneys, produce journal articles, and attract students. Practitioners can help academics reverse these deleterious trends. Practitioners face declining budgets and reduced resources even as citizens demand more and higher-quality services. Many practitioners no longer command the policy research staffs they once did. Governors running for office in the 1990s promised voters they would cut office staff at a time when these experts were most needed. Academics could play a much greater role in public decision making. Under the right circumstances, decision makers would welcome the assistance (see also, Johnson, Frazier, & Riddick, 1983; Sy, 1987).

To play a greater role, academics must understand the limits of their social science to decision makers and must become much more practical in their orientation. This will not be easy: Academics are socialized in opposite ways from decision makers (Goldhamer, 1978; Kaufman, 1995).

RULE 1: KNOW THE LIMITS
OF SOCIAL SCIENCE

Social scientists don't always recognize their discipline's limits, when viewed across the aisle in the political arena. But many observers are beginning to (Pedhazur & Schmelkin, 1991). In the 1970s, many confidently believed their power to crunch numbers with large computers and to reason with sophisticated models would soon eliminate judgment in policy analysis. This misplaced confidence in social science began with Karl Marx and became highly popular in the writings of Karl Mannheim, including *Man and Society in an Age of Reconstruction* (1941), in the 1940s. The late MIT social scientist Donald Schon foresaw the time when models would "be capable of simulating social situations in all their complexity" (Schon, 1983, p. 230). A researcher at the Brookings Institution, Alice Rivlin, later head of President Clinton's Office of Management and Budget, predicted the possibility of modeling America's poverty population to simulate impacts of government policy changes (Rivlin, 1971, p. 35). These hopes proved vain. Human behavior is too complex to model accurately with confidence, and data proved less accessible and reliable than analysts hoped (Frankel, 1973; Winch, 1958). Laws governing human behavior appear to predict less accurately than those governing physical phenomena (Krimerman, 1969). Understanding human behavior remains as much an art as a science (McCloskey, 1985b). Policy analysts differ on answers to such basic questions as, "Would an increase in taxes raise or lower government revenues? Will tight money exorcise the threat of inflation? Would more liberal immigration laws threaten American incomes? Has the distribution of income grown more or less equal over the past thirty years?" (Ulmer, 1984, p. 43).

Modesty now pervades, or should pervade, the social sciences. Social science has become more sophisticated, yet less pretentious (Smelser & Gerstein, 1986). By the 1980s, Schon had revised his earlier optimism, concluding, "Formal models have been usefully employed to solve problems in such relatively undemanding areas as inventory control and logistics. They have generally failed to yield effective results in the more complex, less clearly defined problems of business management, housing policy, or criminal justice" (1983, p. 44). By the late 1970s, a federally convened task force found that "little social research and development is relevant to policy-making, and too much research, even if relevant, is not available to and utilized by appropriate decision-makers" (Lynn, 1978, p. 60). This remains the case at this writing.

Policy analysts could not displace political decision makers, even with better behavioral models (Hamilton, 1992). Political decisions are as much about differences in values and goals as they are about the best way of achieving agreed-upon ends. No amount of analysis can determine whether Congress should approve the North America Free Trade Agreement (NAFTA), although it may persuade policy analysts that there is a "correct" course of action. The political process, not the econometric model, is the best forum for weighing the strength and breadth of pros and cons.

Academic training prepares students for teaching or research, protected from market pressures and to some extent accountability. There are no sanctions or costs to professors for proffering theories or analyses that prove totally wrong or harmful. In a recent article in *The Economist* ("Plenty of Gloom," 1997), the editors reviewed theories calling for environmental catastrophe. None of the doomsayers' predications about food production, population growth, shortages in gas and oil, scarcity of strategic metals, or acid rain proved correct. Ironically, having been so wrong in the past makes these forecasters believe that they will likely be right in the future. The same appears true for stock market forecasters (McGee, 1998). As a result, a great deal of social science has become more and more theoretical and farther and farther away from the real world (Storer, 1966). Students need not understand how the "real world" works. It is enough to manipulate theoretical concepts, mathematical equations, or statistical analysis. They undertake research in arcane, abstract areas for publication in obscure journals most likely to lead professors to tenure (Hawkins, Ritter, & Walter, 1973; Kupfersmid, 1988; Lindsey, 1977). Look in the *Social Science Citation Index*—an annual publication citing who cites articles from other publications—to see that the vast amount of social science publications are referenced by no one.

This perception is so prevalent that in 1998 the governing board of public universities in Massachusetts has as a major goal defunding all social science research. The economist Robert Clower (1995), retiring as editor of the *American Economic Review,* observed that economics would be better off if most articles crossing his desk "had never been written and certainly if most of them hadn't been published" (p. 1). "How," asks economics professor David Colander (1991),

> do economists solve problems without knowledge of the literature of the discipline or institutions? Very abstractly, by referring to models that are not applied to the real world and which cannot be understood by anybody but themselves. That is why most top economic journals look like journals in applied mathematics (Kaufman, 1995). As a result, few, if any, people outside the economics profession can understand the limiting nature of the assumptions that economists make and the irrelevance of much of their work to any real-world problem (see also Stouffer, 1950; Hamilton, 1992). Economists know that much of what they do is simply to elaborate already highly-elaborate mental gymnastics. (p. A52)

Because social scientists lack a sense of their proper roles, lawyers exert more influence on public affairs. Lawyers, not social scientists, monopolize the language of governing. We object.

This need not be. Social scientists as policy analysts know things useful to decision makers (Kaufman, 1995). Academics need to understand that policy analysis reaching decision makers is based on a variety of information, some of it nonscientific, such as anecdotes, metaphor, case studies, advocacy reports, and the like. Policy analysts communicating effectively with decision makers weave this information into decision alternatives for consideration by those in power. Academic experts need to learn to compete. We hope this book shows experts how to inform the decision-making process. We offer social scientists practical ways to make their knowledge available and useful to policymakers. In the long run, social science research will only be useful to decision makers when academics renounce excessive emphasis on theory and develop more practical curricula, or, failing that, at least balance the two (Kaufman, 1995). Departments will reward and promote faculty who practice more applied skills—perhaps even those whose writing can be read, and even enjoyed, by people without PhDs (McCloskey, 1985a,b; Stouffer, 1950; Weiss, 1992).

When social scientists exert caution in interpreting or generalizing their findings, they are responsible to and consistent with professional norms. But decision makers have little use for this policy analysis laden with assumptions and so highly qualified or laid out in vague language that its implications are obscure. Academics need to *package* their policy analysis work differently to appeal to decision makers. This can be done without giving up the rigor of method (Kaufman, 1995). In fact, well-packaged policy work, buttressed by strong science, is in great demand by decision makers (Hamilton, 1992; Kaufman, 1995; Wildavsky, 1979). Unfortunately, quite the opposite might be the case. Alan Binder, in his book, *Hard Heads, Soft Hearts,* offers the "Murphy's Law of Economic Policy: economists have the least influence on policy where they know the most and are agreed; they have the most influence on policy where they know the least and disagree most vehemently" (as quoted in Hamilton, 1992, p. 62).

RULE 2: BE PRACTICAL

We have probably erred in assuming that social problems can be handled in the same way that we manage technological problems. We admit that conflicting interests create hard problems for social policy-makers. But we still underestimate the difficulties in the way of bringing about planned social change, largely because we underestimate the complexity of social systems, of the networks of interaction through which behavior is coordinated in society. . . .
But economic theory, by revealing the interdependence of decisions calls attention to the unexamined consequences of proposals to change. . . . John Maynard Keynes once proposed a toast to economists, "the keepers of the possibility of civilization."

*The possibility of civilization—that is all. The efficient allocation
of resources enlarges the realm of possibilities. A well-coordinated
and smoothly functioning society gives individuals more
opportunity to choose; it does not guarantee that they will choose
well. The economic way of thinking, especially in a democracy, is
an important preliminary. But it is no more than that.*

—Paul T. Heyne, *The Economic Way of Thinking*
(1973, pp. 284-285)

Cost-Benefit Analysis and Policy Analysis

When social scientists analyze policy issues—from health care cost
containment through long-term poverty to pollution abatement and
crime—many prefer cost-benefit analysis, the flagship of analytic methods
(MacRae & Whittington, 1997). Cost-benefit analysis promulgates invaluable rules for identifying beneficial outcomes and costs resulting from
policy decisions. It also lays out rules for comparing those benefits and
costs. It allows analysts to rank policies as solutions to clearly defined
problems: What, for example, are the expenses and values of conserving
water leaking from a mud-lined irrigation canal by lining the canal with
concrete or installing pumps to extract seepage water?

But few public policy problems or their solutions are so clearly defined.
Cost-benefit analysis is not policy analysis as understood by decision
makers or by policy analysts who are effective in communicating with
them. Decision makers rarely ask experts to calculate relative merits of a
few measurable alternatives. They are much more likely to ask experts to
find ways of dealing with drought, falling middle-class incomes, or rising
crime rates—problems dumped on politicians' desks by anxious voters,
ambitious editorial writers, or well-organized special interest or advocacy
groups. Before applying their elegant technical skills to produce answers,
experts must figure out what the questions are.

Cost-benefit analysis leaves out the four most difficult steps in the more
practical view of policy analysis (see also, MacRae & Whittington, 1997;
Squire & van der Tak, 1975; Ward & Deren, 1991):

- Defining the problem (Are more people on welfare or are the same number
  of people on welfare but for longer periods?)
- Diagnosing causes (Are low test scores in schools the result of deteriorating performance of students or are more students with lesser abilities
  taking tests?)

- Identifying potential solutions (What programs could help people get off welfare?)
- Communicating new policies (How can taxpayers be convinced that reforms will cut welfare rolls and not inflate the bureaucracy?)

Cost-benefit analysis, as is the case with most social science policy research methods, assumes a predictable and structured environment for answering questions. Policy analysis in the policy arena, on the other hand, is usually conducted amid noise, confusion, and urgency. Practical policy analysis uses cost-benefit analysis, but only as one of many sources of information.

Policy Analysis and Medicine Compared

Analyzing policy is more akin to diagnosing patients in a hospital emergency room than to performing elaborate statistical calculations. Medical diagnosis depends heavily on physicians' judgment and experience as well as technical competence. It also depends on having reliable diagnostic equipment and sufficient time available for the task: Diagnostic practices in a wartime field hospital differ from those employed in a prestigious private clinic. Policy analysis must usually follow procedures more like those used in the former than in the latter.

Both physicians and policy analysts must be well grounded in theoretical foundations. But theory is not enough. After all, possible causes of and treatments for patients' conditions may be too numerous to be examined one after another. Physicians and policy analysts must often diagnose and prescribe before they can test all theoretical possibilities. Patients can die, and economic problems become crises, while physicians or analysts run through comprehensive tests.

There are, of course, important differences between medical practice and policy analysis. On the whole, physicians have an easier time of it. Medicine has developed simple, although in some cases expensive, tests to identify many diseases or injuries: Medical researchers watch under a microscope while bacteria wither before antibiotics. Policy analysts often cannot experiment. Few decision makers are willing to withhold treatment from one group to see how effective it is for another. They can never know whether or how political actions relate to economic and social outcomes. While physicians learn through textbooks and practical internships focusing on the treatment of disease, social scientists study and develop theories about how societies or economies work. Policy analysts in academe inhabit a world characterized by omniscience, equilibrium, and frictionless adjustments. Yet, politicians wrestle daily with problems caused by ignorance, trauma, and friction, often of their own making.

Few experienced decision makers would find the medical analogy far-fetched. Physicians and policymakers both face rooms full of patients—some self-admitted, others referred by other physicians, and still others brought in by ambulance. Etiology is often unknown and prognosis difficult. Patients must be managed with too few staff and too little time. Errors are easily made and consequences grave. Under the Ford administration, for instance, health officials approved a hastily prepared vaccine for the swine flu. Not only was the vaccine unnecessary, it killed more Americans than the flu when administered. To make fewer mistakes, physicians follow three steps: (a) carefully identify the patient's symptoms and note signs, (b) systematically rule out inappropriate causes to arrive at the most likely diagnosis, and (c) judiciously select appropriate treatments. Then, they (d) predict likely outcomes; (e) review their work through quality assurance; and (f) throughout, figure out what to say and how to say it.

1. Symptomatology

Sir William Osler, the great 19th-century British surgeon, believed physicians should make initial assessments by stating first what you see and not by touching the patient (Bryan, 1997). Good advice for the policy analyst. An objective problem description—that is, one in which biases from all sources are understood (Kaplan, 1964)—unclouded by the patient's views or those of patient advocates, is the best foundation for accurate diagnosis.

But objective information in the political arena is hard to find. In fact, it cannot exist even in science (Nagel, 1961; Scriven, 1983). Many people distort information—sometimes inadvertently, more often deliberately, sometimes with the best of intentions, often for personal gain, occasionally to discredit. Others withhold information. In 1974, for example, owners of domestic oil reserves depicted the price hikes of the Organization of Petroleum Exporting Countries (OPEC) as the consequence of U.S. dependence on foreign oil. After all, if oil imports were restricted, the value of domestic supplies would increase. In the same way, the real estate industry argued in 1985 that America faced a crisis of affordable housing and that the federal government should help would-be home owners—a boost to housing sales and real estate agents' commissions. And teachers made "education reform" a national priority because public concern commanded smaller classes and higher salaries.

To be accurate, withholding data is often a good thing. Milton Friedman (1998, p. 36) recalled that Hong Kong's British financial secretary, John

Cowperthwaite, in the 1960s forbade the gathering of too much economic data to prevent planners from using it to ruin the colony's miracle economy. Withholding policy-relevant information for strategic or tactical use is endemic in the policy arena. Officials in deregulated savings and loans withheld data on poorly performing loans, and bank regulators neglected to ask for them, precipitating a multibillion-dollar financial crisis in the 1980s. Asian banks, especially in Japan and South Korea, followed much the same path in the 1990s, leading to a world crisis in stock markets ("East Asia," 1998).

The policy analyst's first job, therefore, is to prepare a disinterested assessment of the problem—stripping away distortions and filling in gaps by drawing from a wide range of sources. The object is not to make information objective but to clearly understand its biases by bringing additional information to bear. How to do this is covered in Chapter 2.

2. Diagnostics

Physicians and policy analysts diagnose problems armed with objective descriptions. Good diagnosis depends on forming competing hypotheses consistent with signs and symptoms and on developing analysis to identify the hypothesis best fitting the circumstances. In the rush to help, physicians and decision makers may hasten to find one plausible hypothesis, then muster as much supporting evidence as statistics allow. Experts, for example, try to explain rising numbers of homeless people in terms of cutbacks in social programs and mass unemployment—overlooking impacts of state mental hospital closings, demolition of single-room-only hotels, and increases in substance abuse. Others were quick to interpret rising unemployment in the steel industry in the early 1980s as evidence of declining "competitiveness" of U.S. companies in world markets—overlooking the inevitable structural shifts in expanded world trade; implications of past monopolistic practices; adoption of new technologies; rising costs of pollution abatement; and corporate asset-stripping, merging, and downsizing (Buss & Redburn, 1983).

Good policy analysts, therefore, are not necessarily the first to come up with plausible explanations. Rather, they offer the best evidence in support of the chosen diagnosis as well as the best reasons for rejecting alternative explanations.

Identification of causes, not just signs and symptoms, is critical. Policy intervention, to be effective, must get at the cause of the problem (MacRae & Whittington, 1997).

Looking at different causes creates different hypotheses for assessment (Stinchcombe, 1968). Some problems originate from actions of private institutions or individuals—careless or criminal disposal of toxic waste, for example. Others result from public agency intervention—failure of a retraining program to place graduates in jobs. Some problems arise from systemic issues—absence of liability laws associated with waste disposal. Others are unique, or, at least, rare events—violation of waste disposal laws. Systemic problems may require policies that alter decision making. Nonsystemic problems may simply require public action to deal with the consequences. Chapter 3 describes diagnostic techniques for policy analysts.

3. Prescription

Diagnosis is the basis for, but does not determine, prescription. Physicians cannot treat patients until they assess other aspects of their condition. A surgeon sometimes undertakes an operation on young or middle-aged patients that could not be safely performed on older patients, and drugs can be prescribed only if the patient is unlikely to suffer an adverse reaction.

For decision makers, the obvious prescription may not be the best. Obvious prescriptions are usually attempts by interest groups to tilt the public cornucopia their way. The economist Mancur Olson describes this perpetual tug-of-war as *rent-seeking* (Amacher and Ulbrich, 1986; Olson, 1965). Government decisions—to change the tax code, provide subsidies, tinker with trade rules—bestow benefits, or rents, on regions, industries, or groups. These benefits are paid for by the general public. Dairy price supports, for example, transfer money from everyone buying milk to the few farmers raising cows. In the case of the homeless mentally ill, decision makers concluded that the treatment was worse than the disease. In the 1960s, homeless mentally ill people were often committed to state mental hospitals on the authority of a physician's signature. There was little or no process. Many suffered untold horrors in state facilities. Now, homeless mentally ill people have due process rights making it difficult to involuntarily institutionalize or detain them, even for their own protection. Although usually couched in terms of the national interest, at heart, policy debates concern rents. The good policy analyst understands how government creates rents and how groups avidly pursue them. Chapter 4 lays out rules for designing policy prescriptions.

The human body includes complex self-healing mechanisms. Yet, physicians, who usually do little more than modestly aid the body in its natural healing, often enjoy patients' gratitude more properly due to nature. Good decision makers know that the body politic also includes self-correcting mechanisms capable of dealing with most problems. But they need voters' gratitude at the next election. Physicians and decision makers must appear to be healers to retain their patients' trust and confidence. The appearance of inaction, however defensible, wins few thanks. Whereas physicians may enjoy monopolies on treating patients (a second opinion is traditionally supportive of the first), decision makers must compete for the position of healer. The chief executive, legislators, political wannabes, and special interest groups all claim to know best how to solve problems. So, decision makers must often act simply to avoid the appearance of inaction. They rarely have the luxury of doing nothing, however preferred from a social scientific standpoint. Hence, the importance of the Hippocratic oath warning physicians "at least, should do no harm." Sir William Osler recognized physicians' propensity to meddle when he described the physician's duty to teach patients not to rely on medicine—an injunction more honored in the breach than in the observance both by physicians and decision maker counterparts (Bryan, 1997). For decision makers the preferred method of acting without doing so is appointing a *task force* of all stakeholders. By the time these people resolve their differences and issue a report, no one will care.

Good decisions aren't those that look good in hindsight. They are those in the present best defended against alternatives not selected. Anyone can be a policy wizard with the advantage of hindsight. Policy analysts are likely to find the best solution with fewer serious errors if they rank alternative prescriptions. Criteria for ranking depend on problem assessment, administrative priorities, political and economic environment, and many other factors, as well as measurable costs and benefits.

4. Prognostication and Evaluation

Like a physician's prognostication, policy is made prospectively—based on assumptions about how economic and social conditions change and how government actions influence. This requires forecasts drawing on an eclectic mixture of formal models and informal prediction. Chapter 5 puts forecasting in perspective.

Although costs and benefits can be precisely weighted, using rules laid out in Chapter 6, sorting out what makes sense in politics is an art. Academics like to identify the "best" course of action by comparing expected results with expectations had no action been taken. Yet, academics overlook how personality, politics, and the institutional design of public agencies influence policy analysis and decision-making effectiveness. Budget cycles, laws and regulations, civil service procedures, and legislative time limits determine policy and program success or failure. Academics conceive of time as a distant horizon toward which the present unfolds smoothly. But political time horizons are shorter and the journey toward them is interrupted by deadlines and unpredictable events.

5. Communication

Policy analysts must clearly communicate ideas to decision makers. Both elected and appointed officials generally are not technical experts. They don't want information conveyed in academic prose. But they need to know more than which option yields the highest "present value." They must weigh politics as well as economics. They need to know what assumptions the policy analyst made, what information is missing, and who gains and loses (Lasswell, 1971). Good policy analysis highlights relevant information for decision makers; it does *not* make those decisions.

Social scientists learn or prefer to only communicate with one another (Frey & Eichenberger, 1993; McCloskey, 1985b; Stouffer, 1950). The academic journal article is too arcane, too disorganized, too complex, too irrelevant, and usually covered with too many caveats to be useful (Kitcher, 1985). Most journal articles are difficult to read (Halpert, 1990). The last two chapters of this book offer rules for communicating technical information to decision makers, the analog of conferring with a patient, consulting with a specialist, or preparing progress notes on patient records. Chapter 7 describes how analysts can decide what to communicate: Analysts can't relate all they know because decision makers have neither the expertise nor the time to digest everything. Although academics may take professional pride in complex research, they cannot tell others their findings until they have, in the words of Alain Enthoven (1974), "come out of the other side and are able to explain the essentials of the problem in clear and understandable terms" (p. 459). Experts unable to explain their ideas to busy but interested nonexperts have not truly mastered their subject.

Chapter 8 offers rules for clear writing. The transition from academic to practical policy analyst is not easy. Decision makers ignore or misrepresent advice, and silence or disparage advisors. In each chapter, we outline rules for examining and reporting policy issues. Some might argue that the medical analogy breaks down at this point: Physicians are notorious for lacking writing skills, even penmanship. But anyone reading reports in bureaucratese would have trouble distinguishing the two. Our point: We can always do better.

We also provide examples, many drawn from our own experiences. We do not try to relate either rules or examples to social science theory or academic policy analysis methods; we include only an occasional figure or table. Instead, we offer practical guidelines to the thousands of people involved in public policy either as academics or practitioners.

Steven Rhoads (1985), in an excellent book on the role of economics in public policy, concluded,

> Good politicians will want advice that assesses policy proposals on their substantive merits, but good politicians, of course, must consider political strategy and tactics as well. They will want to weigh questions of timing and sponsorship. They may support policy they think is substantively bad in order to head off political pressure for one they think is even worse. Alternatively, they may fail to support a substantively good policy because they believe that the legislative struggle for passage will hurt the prospects of still more important parts of their programs. Good politics thus requires both finding good answers to substantive policy questions and strategic and tactical skill. Although both parts are important, economists concern themselves only with policy substance. (p. 8)

SUMMARY

In spite of their differences, academic experts and public decision-makers need one another: Academics would like to communicate what they know to decision makers and decision makers would like the best information available for decision making. Academics can effectively insinuate their ideas into politics if they (a) understand the limits of social science policy research from the perspective of politicians and competitors, and (b) package their work in a much more practical way. Academics must realize that social science, as usually practiced, is limited in its capacity to address policy issues public officials care about. Social science policy research tends to be too theoretical, esoteric, or trivial, and irrelevant and speculative, not to mention biased. Social scientists tend to hold grand visions for what their science can accomplish; practitioners do not. Social science policy research must offer decision makers viable alternatives for decision making if it is to be useful and compete with policy information from other sources—bureaucracy, think tanks, advocacy groups, mass media. Social scientists must also make their work more practical. One way to do this is to apply the medical model to policy analysis. Policy analysts, like physicians, must (a) assess signs and symptoms of problems, (b) develop a problem diagnosis carefully identifying causes and effects, (c) lay out prescriptions for treatment so that the most effective can be selected, (d) forecast and evaluate, and (e) communicate. Unlike social science policy researchers, analysts must look at politics, timing, and sponsorship.

2

Assessing

The executive branch, however it is organized, obeys no coherent set of goals or objectives. The responsibilities assigned to the government are not the single product of one well-organized mind. They are the cumulative debris of legislative battles, court compromises, interest group demands, bureaucratic tradition, and federal mandates. Each one has an organization counterpart, and each organization or sub organization has its own constituency. Few of these are as concerned about the overall architecture or government as they are with the narrow sliver of the public interest they believe they represent. All respect the governorship in abstract and all treat the governor with deference, but none rely on the governor to furnish them with an agenda.

—Thad L. Beyle and Lynn Muchmore,
Being Governor: The View From the Office (1983, p. 10)

Policy problems are rarely what they seem. Growing numbers of homeless people may be depicted as victims of mass unemployment; the rising number of small business failures may appear a symptom of a "credit squeeze" imposed by unsympathetic bankers; or surging unemployment may be blamed on inadequate social services following a plant closing.

But each problem turns out to be very different from its initial presentation—however plausible. Competition among interest groups or issue advocates for decision makers' attention causes confusion. These groups often have good intentions. They believe their cause to be just and their view correct. But they must compete among themselves for attention in an environment where the electoral process and expectations conjured by the mass media create artificial crises and distorted time horizons. This hot world of public decision-making is far from the cool world of academe.

Policy analysts operate in an environment every bit as confused as an urban hospital's emergency room on a Saturday night. Just as physicians employ protocols that let them concentrate on those most urgently needing

14

care, policy analysts must use common sense to best allocate their time and energy. This chapter offers simple rules of thumb for practical policy analysts confronted with a bewildering number of issues, all clamoring for attention.

RULE 1: MAINTAIN AN OPEN MIND

Sherlock Holmes was fond of warning Dr. Watson not to theorize until he had gathered the facts. It's good advice for policy analysts too. Don't believe issue characterizations either by opponents or proponents until you've checked the facts yourself. And don't check the facts until, as far as possible, you've eliminated—or at least become aware of—your own preconceptions. We all have biases. Most of us, however, like to think of our biases as judgment or experience.

In public policy, as in medicine, good information is the foundation of successful action. But good information can be rare in both situations: Facts are elusive, reasoning is absent, and disinterested witnesses nonexistent. Therefore, policy analysts, like medical researchers, must maintain an open mind, doubting views, however plausible and widely held, until they have carefully examined the evidence. And they must employ their own trusted sources to secure necessary information. In general, the more sources the better.

A great part of the information obtained is contradictory, a still greater part is false, and by far the greatest part is doubtful. What is required is a certain power of discrimination, which only knowledge of human behavior and good judgment can bring.

Experienced politicians recognize the problematic nature of policy-relevant information. A town hit with a plant closing exaggerates its plight to attract aid from state or federal government (Buss & Vaughan, 1988). Local governments overstate wastewater financing needs to gain approval for placement of a bond issue on the ballot (Apogee Associates, 1987). And social welfare agencies inflate caseloads to justify budget increases (Buss & Vaughan, 1989). *Factoids*—assertions that sound plausible, that appeal to our emotions, and that the news media treat as established truths—infest public issues. But factoids have no basis in fact. They are artificial, creations of people trying to shape policy debates.

Consider three factoids:

Factoid 1. In 1977, steel plant closings devastated Youngstown, Ohio (Buss & Redburn, 1983). Decision makers equated the problem with a natural disaster: The community's economic base had been destroyed and people would need help to survive the trauma. Yet, the real problem was very different. The community was experiencing a rapid shift from steel production toward a service-based economy. Local human service agencies lacked flexibility, not capacity, to serve displaced workers well (Buss & Vaughan, 1988). But the city's economy persevered and few steelworkers used the network of expensive programs intended to help them.

Factoid 2. In the mid-1980s, the question of whether low-income people could afford housing emerged as a top priority. The median price of homes sold had risen to $93,000, far above the means of most first-time home buyers. The president and Congress prepared programs to make homes affordable. But the inability to afford housing was a factoid. First-time home buyers do not buy median-priced homes, so they didn't face prices of $93,000. Prices rose because the average age of sellers and buyers increased as baby boomers moved into larger and better housing. Adjusted for changes in quality, the price of housing increased more slowly than inflation (falling in real terms), and the cost of home ownership—including interest rates on home mortgages—fell after 1982 (Case, 1989).

Factoid 3. Under growing public pressure to address America's homeless problem, the U.S. Department of Housing and Urban Development (HUD) conducted an unprecedented study to estimate the number of homeless people nationwide (Redburn & Buss, 1986). Using a variety of research methods looking for convergence, HUD estimated that on any given night, between 150,000 to 350,000 people were homeless. In subsequent studies, researchers found no more than 700,000 homeless people. Such low estimates devastated the homeless advocacy community, because it meant that much-hoped-for federal aid would not be forthcoming. In response, the homeless advocate and Washington, D.C., shelter operator Mitch Snyder held a news conference denouncing HUD and offering 2 million as the correct number of homeless people. At subsequent news conferences, Snyder raised the number to 3 million. Snyder also sued HUD and individual researchers over the numbers. Subsequent examinations of Snyder's estimates showed them to be pure fabrication—factoids. Yet, every winter, the news media dutifully report that several million people go to sleep homeless every night.

The analyst's first task is to question problem characterizations. Ask where numbers come from, carefully exploring the logic underlying factoids. This seems heartless—akin to denying help to the needy. Advocacy groups and politicians who disagree with policy analysis are more than willing to point this out as a way to discredit what they don't like. It seems plausible that unemployed people need social services, that poorly housed people need cheap houses, and that 10 times more shelters and soup kitchens are necessary.

Not so. In fact, if we were to offer prescriptions that follow logically from these depictions—psychiatric counseling for the unemployed, subsidies to the construction industry, and massive increases in assistance to homeless people—we would spend a lot of public money without necessarily helping those in need. The unemployed need help, but only a few benefit from psychiatric counseling. The homeless also need help, probably the least of which is cheap housing. Those with histories of substance abuse, psychiatric problems, physical and mental disability, and no social support network, not to mention lack of skills in demand in the labor market, benefit little from shelters, except perhaps in emergencies. Even then, homeless people avoid shelters out of fear of assault or theft, and in some cases out of dislike of religious proselytizing.

Being skeptical is not the same as being cynical. Skepticism simply recognizes that, in the complex political arena, facts may be distorted. Cynicism ascribes the worst possible motive—and is likely to be wrong as often as a naïveté that accepts everything at face value.

The policy consultant William Nothdurft (1988) believes questions most likely to separate facts from factoids are, So what? How much? and Who says? Apply them to the factoids above. Ask "so what" and we pinpoint what's at stake. In Factoid 1, the stake is in people's ability to cope with job loss. What help do they need?

But this is not the process decision makers always follow. Instead, they often ask agency directors what the unemployed need. Administrators, unfortunately, have a vested interest in defining needs in terms of services their agencies offer. If you hold a hammer in your hand, goes the saying attributed to philosopher Abraham Kaplan, then everything starts to look like a nail (Kaplan, 1964). In Youngstown's steel crisis, for example, virtually every agency, regardless of its mission, tried to make a case for receiving state and federal funding. A Latino social service agency lobbied successfully for funding to establish an emergency psychiatric service for steelworkers requiring the services of a Spanish-speaking psychiatrist. This in spite of the fact that only a handful of Latinos worked in the mills. As epilogue, not one steelworker used this service. Asking "so what" about housing affordability invites a focus on inadequate incomes of families crowded in dilapidated housing. We quickly redefine the issue as lack of income, not over-priced housing. For the homeless, the issue becomes more shelter space, gainsaying social services necessary to really help them. Ask "how much" and we must reevaluate the problem's importance. How many unemployed people lined up for counseling services? How many failed to pay mortgages on time? How many abused spouses? Actual data from communities where plants closed show that very few laid-off people made use of the services agency directors claimed they would need. Ask how many badly housed people could take advantage of cheap housing if it were available and the answer is also, "Very few." Look at independent evaluations of the McKinney Act programs for the homeless and conclude that the social service system has failed to address the homeless problem.

Ask "who says" and we learn why problems have been misrepresented. We discover how managers of social service agencies defined the needs of the unemployed often without asking the unemployed themselves. We also find that realtors discovered the lack of affordable housing. Advocates for the homeless forced the action to discover them. We should always balance social service agency portrayals of problems with independent studies by researchers without a vested interest in program funding or outcomes. This is an area where policy analysts in academe have a decided market advantage. They need to exploit it better.

Too many journalists take problem assessments straight from press releases prepared by interested parties. The few who dig a little deeper find interesting stories. The *New Republic* writer Mickey Kaus (1992) examined facts widely repeated during the 1992 presidential campaign. One was the allegation, repeated on the CBS evening news, that "a startling number of American children [are] in danger of starving. . . . One out of eight American children under the age of 12 is going hungry tonight." Kaus concluded,

> It's crap. [Dan] Rather misreports a "study" by the Food Research and Action Center, a Washington organization that lobbies for government food aid. The study did not measure malnutrition, much less starvation. It purports to identify children whose families were strapped for cash to buy food at any time over the previous year (not each night). Low-income people were asked eight "key questions," some of which might draw affirmative responses from Donald Trump (e.g.: "Do your children ever say they are hungry because there is not enough food in the house?"). Those answering yes to five of the eight questions were pro-

nounced "hungry." Those giving even one "yes" were deemed "at risk" of hunger. (p. 24)

Alain Enthoven, advisor to Defense Secretary Robert MacNamara, estimated that asking the right question was 90% of an analyst's job (Zeckhauser, 1974). It is also one of the least emphasized aspects of the policy analysis enterprise. It is only by asking questions that we can hope to understand what the problem really is. As the Duke of Wellington observed, "The business of war, indeed, the whole business of life, is to discover what we do not know from what we do know" (quoted in Hibbert, 1997, p. 123).

RULE 2: LOOK BEHIND THE NUMBERS

Numbers mislead easily and often. Publishing a number in official documents does not make it true. Neither does truth reside in professional journal articles by virtue of their having been refereed and printed. Pinned on the wall in the UK Central Statistical Office is a card reading: "Any figure that looks interesting is probably wrong." Analysts can avoid the seduction of quantification.

First, find out who compiled the data and beware of impressive names. Statistics are nowhere near as objective as statisticians make out. The British Prime Minister Benjamin Disraeli claimed there were "lies, damned lies, and statistics." Interest groups tend to create their own research centers to influence public policy. The National Center for Research on [your topic here] may sound like a high-powered and objective organization. It may not be. The picture of large numbers of undernourished American children, described above, was painstakingly built up from results of seven small, unrepresentative surveys. Local advocacy groups such as the Alabama Coalition Against Hunger—interested in getting "yes" answers to questions on poor nutrition—conducted surveys. Kraft General Foods, a major corporate beneficiary of federal food subsidies, financed them. Even the names of prestigious universities are often attached to research reports they had little role in preparing. (It is common practice in academe to use one's university affiliation when engaging in private consulting. This may vet consulting reports not endorsed by the university [see, e.g., General Accounting Office (GAO), 1986].) Just because a vested interest group publishes a research report should not be grounds for rejecting the report outright. But savvy policy analysts will see red flags with interest group involvement, even when they may agree with that group's perspective. *Caution* is the watchword.

Second, know how data are compiled. All data have eccentricities, sometimes associated with definitions (Alonzo & Starr, 1987; Frumkin, 1987; Maier, 1991; Rubenstein, 1994). If a man marries his housekeeper or cook and does not pay his new wife for her services, the measured national income falls, although the value of goods and services produced remains unchanged. Other eccentricities result from deliberate manipulation by data providers. A community health center justified a budget request to help displaced workers by reporting a large increase in the numbers of displaced workers seeking help. When researchers examined the cases carefully, they found agency administrators had lied: They counted not only displaced workers but nonworking family members, including children (Buss & Vaughan, 1988).

Remember, even official statistics have humble origins. The noted British statistician Sir Josiah Stamp commented that whatever wonders experts performed with statistices, one must not forget that the figures came initially from someone like a village watchman, who recorded what he pleased.

Policy analysts can only know what numbers really mean if they read the small print in footnotes below statistical tables, in appendices, or in referenced publications. Do *transfer payments* in government income statistics include farm subsidy payments? What do people have to do to be counted as unemployed? What sort of businesses are counted in business failure rates? What is a discouraged worker? What does it mean to be homeless? The fine print in government reports often provides quite revealing insights into data interpretation. Ignore these in policy analysis at your own peril.

But even careful reading of statistical documents is unlikely to expose conceptual flaws in data. Consider two widely used economic statistics during the 1980s: the declining rate of growth of America's gross domestic product, leading to the widespread belief that the economy was in crisis; and the yawning balance of payments deficit, fostering the belief that American businesses could no longer compete with their foreign rivals (Krugman, 1994, 1996).

Although widely accepted, both numbers were wildly misleading. The apparent sluggish economy was, for the most part, an illusion. It was created by difficulties in adjusting official output statistics for improvements in the quality of goods and services—especially of services. It's easier to measure more of something than to measure a better something. According to government statistics, there was virtually no increase in output per service employee during the 1980s, whereas the output per goods-producing employee grew by a healthy 2.9% each year. Examine how output is measured in key service industries. The annual value of freight transportation, for example, is number of tons carried multiplied by number of miles traveled. As computers improved freight dispatching, customers got better, faster hauling of freight. But, because ton-miles falls, economic data reflect a fall in output. Furthermore, with deregulation of interstate freight hauling after 1978, the number of truckers needed to ship the nation's road freight fell dramatically. Looking at employment growth would give quite the wrong impression of sector activity.

Another example: The number of checks processed and deposits accepted measure a part of the annual value of banking output. The value of cash dispensers and electronic funds transfers is understated. "Conceptual problems in measuring output in services are compounded by the paucity of data," points out *The Economist*.

> Although the service sector accounts for almost three-quarters of America's GDP [gross domestic product], official number-crunchers collect far more figures on manufacturing industry. Government statistics on footwear, for instance, are broken down into unbelievable detail: men's and women's shoes, slippers, running shoes, etc. Figures on restaurants lump MacDonalds [*sic*] together with the Four Seasons. ("American Growth," 1992, p. 91)

Statisticians collect numbers that are easy to gather, not necessarily numbers that really matter. Adjust economic statistics for quality and price, *The Economist* continues, and growth per employee during the 1980s was at least comparable to growth in the first 80 years of this century, if not stronger.

On top of the quality problem, changing relative prices muddle aggregate data. Because computer prices plummeted during the 1980s, their share of production in manufacturing shrank. If output data recorded memory capacity or computational speed, instead of numbers of computers sold, we would have a very different picture of sectoral growth (Darby, 1992).

America's intractable trade deficit was the decade's most persistent economic story. "Competitiveness" became a watchword for Washington policymakers. Unfortunately, trade data are no more reliable than productivity data. Again, the problem is caused by the rapid growth of services. Although the U.S. Department of Commerce collects fairly accurate data on shipments of goods into and out of the United States, it has no way of collecting data on the value of services sold to foreigners by America's lawyers, technical consultants, hospitals, and universities. Trade figures also make no allowance for sales among American-owned subsidiaries of American businesses. Should the United States count as an import the shipments from a General Motors Mexican subsidiary to a plant in the north? Some researchers estimate that allowing for this invisible component of our trade balance in 1993 converts a deficit into a surplus as high as $140 billion.

And consider how Mickey Kaus (1992) deflated two more popular statistical myths:

> Real, after-tax income fell for most American families in the 1980s. Nope. [T]his statistic (used by William Raspberry and *Time*, among others) is a bit too bad to be true. One problem comes in measuring income by "families." Families are getting smaller. A couple with one child living on $30,000 in 1990 is a lot better off financially than a family of six trying to make do on the same real income in 1950. When the Congressional Budget Office corrects for these shifts, the bottom 40 percent (not "most") of the population has lost ground since 1977. But significantly (for Democrats, anyway) the bulk of the damage occurred before 1980. In the much maligned '80s, the top 70 percent of families gained, with or without the CBO adjustments. Sorry.
>
> *Average weekly earnings in America today are lower than they were in the last week that Dwight Eisenhower was President.* If this "stat-bite" from Senator Daniel Patrick Moynihan is true, the country's really gone to hell. But it isn't true. Moynihan uses data from the Bureau of Labor Statistics for "production and non-supervisory workers." The BLS survey is screwy, in part because it measures a smaller and smaller segment of the labor force as the economy shifts to white-collar work. Figures for the entire work force, from more reliable Social Security records, show an average 30 percent gain since Ike's day.
>
> Third, beware of specious accuracy. A statistician, according to a cynical adage, is someone who draws a precise line from an unwarranted assumption to a foregone conclusion. With all the problems inherent in social science research, analysts may be so gratified to achieve a statistically significant result that they report it in all its cumbersome detail. When you catch yourself putting two or three numbers after a decimal point on a decision memorandum, ask if the issue merits such accuracy. An old joke worth remembering when failing to round off numbers: Economists use decimal points just to show they have a sense of humor. (p. 7)

In his classic 1954 book, *How to Lie with Statistics*, Darrell Huff quotes a *Time* magazine report: "The average Yaleman, Class of '24, makes $25,111 a year." Huff was alarmed by this number: "It is surprisingly precise. It is quite improbably salubrious" (p. 11). He raises three problems with claims on behalf of Yale men: (a) It was improbable that anyone knew last year's income to the nearest dollar so precisely unless it was all salary—and few $25,000 annual incomes in 1954 were all salary. (b) The high average is based on what respondents said they earned—and some would have exaggerated out of vanity or optimism. (c) Sample respondents to the question about how much they earned is skewed toward those who could be easily traced by the university and who were prepared to answer a mail survey. Those not questioned or who tore up the survey may have earned much less than those who answered. Precise numbers give a false sense of what we really know.

Fourth, check age of the data. Some grocery and pharmaceutical packages carry dates after which the contents may be spoiled. Numbers don't— although they should. Many numbers are old when published and even older before analysis. Frustrated policy analysts struggle with census data up to 10 years old before new data are available. Decision makers often debate the economy as it was several years ago. Presidents and Congresses argue over how to stimulate the national economy years after the passage of the recession's trough. The chairman of the Federal Reserve Board, Alan Greenspan, in a speech to economists in January 1998, lamented that his job was to stabilize prices, but by the time he has the data to regulate the money supply, they're too old to be of use (*All Things Considered,* 1998).

An example of the influence of obsolete data was the fashion for states to set up public finance agencies during the early 1980s (Vaughan, Pollard, & Dyer, 1984). These new bureaucracies filled gaps believed to exist in venture capital availability for new, high-technology businesses in early growth phases. States accepted without question evidence showing that private flows of venture capital had dried up. In fact, the venture capital shortage had ended in 1978 when financial regulations and tax laws were changed to reverse biases against risk. By the time the states acted, the venture capital spigot was wide open again. Had policy analysts taken trouble to look at more recent data—which were readily available—they may have questioned the need for new public venture capital programs.

Fifth, don't confuse statistical significance with policy significance. Huff (1954) was fond of saying, "A difference is a difference only if it makes a difference" (p. 58). Social science research is grounded in hypothesis testing to determine statistical significance. If not statistically significant, study results are rejected. If statistically significant, they are accepted. Too often, policy analysts and decision makers confuse statistical significance with policy significance: Results that are not statistically significant can have major policy implications, whereas those that are statistically significant may have no policy implications (see also, Tukey, 1969). For example, researchers may report that there is no statistically significant difference between the health status of immigrants and citizens while failing to realize that the sheer number of unhealthy immigrants is itself a public health problem. By contrast, researchers may report that women starting new businesses are less likely to receive bank financing then their male counterparts, not seeing that the percentage difference between the two is so small that no public intervention—say, a public subsidy program for women—is needed.

Ask: Compared to what? A popular way to use numbers in a misleading way is to leave them floating—without a basis for comparison. After a thick London smog in 1952, Britain's Ministry of Health reported that 2,800 people died. A shocked Parliament enacted strict new laws requiring households to burn only smokeless coal and offering financial incentives to switch to electric heating. Yet, how lethal was the smog? Later reports showed that the additional 2,800 people portrayed as casualties were mostly elderly with severe respiratory problems. Many would have lived for only a short time even breathing the cleanest air. The deaths, therefore, represented a small increase in overall mortality. Smog abatement may have been a wise move, but the sensational body count should not have been the basis for action.

Ask if the numbers make sense. It's better to be roughly right by applying common sense than exactly wrong by applying complex statistics. For example, when OPEC drove up oil prices in 1973, Congress commissioned a study to determine whether people would reduce gas consumption voluntarily as prices rose or whether rationing would be the only way to allocate scarce gasoline supplies. Researchers analyzed the relationship between gasoline use and prices nationwide after World War II. But the period was one during which gasoline prices had fallen in real terms, subject to minor fluctuations. Not surprising, statistical models found little relationship between price and consumption—the effects of minor changes were swamped by the influence of long-term decline in prices, rising incomes, bigger cars, and many other factors. Researchers falsely concluded that people were insensitive to gasoline price and consumption, leading to the disastrous rationing experiment in early 1974, with long lines and angry drivers. During the next 10 years, however, confronted with a large and apparently permanent change in energy prices, people cut energy use quickly and dramatically. Numbers suggesting that people consistently act erroneously or against their own long-term interests should be treated with some skepticism.

Theory and empirical evidence can lead us to go wrong with confidence. The late George Stigler (1988) said,

At leading centers of economic theory . . . it has been the practice to ask: Is the new theory logically correct? That is a good question but not as good as a second question: Does the new theory help us understand observable economic life? No one will deny the desirability of eventually answering the second question, but many economists prefer to leave that question for a later time and a different person to answer. That division of labor is quite proper, but until the second question is answered a theory has no standing and, therefore, should not be used as a guide to public policy. (p. 20)

Despite the benefits of economic thinking, social scientists should never let theory and mathematics overwhelm common sense (see, e.g., Hahn & Litan, 1997). Fortunately, analysts have several books about the strengths and weaknesses of government statistics available (see, especially, Alonzo & Starr, 1987; Frumkin, 1987; Maier, 1991). A basic guide belongs in every policy analyst's desk library.

RULE 3: LEARN THE HISTORY OF THE ISSUE

I have come across men of letters who have written history without taking part in public affairs, and politicians who have concerned themselves with producing events without thinking about them. I have observed that the first are always inclined to find general causes, whereas the second, living in the midst of disconnected daily facts, are prone to imagine that everything is attributable to particular incidents, and that the wires they pull are the same as those that move the world. It is to be presumed that both are equally deceived.
—Alexis de Tocqueville, *Democracy in America* (1848)

The most important qualification to be a good seer, so the adage runs, is a long memory. Memory matters for policy analysts too. History offers powerful lessons to explain the future. It also places contemporary problems in perspective. "Learning the history of an issue can help the analyst understand both the economics and the politics of its current incarnation," claims James Verdier (1984, p. 422), an analyst at the Congressional Budget Office.

Learning an issue's background is as important to policy analysis as learning a patient's medical history is to a physician. It reduces the chances of making a diagnostic error. Well-informed analysts are less likely to succumb to the time-saving temptation to treat issues as generic examples of familiar, but not necessarily similar, problems.

If the problem is growing welfare caseloads, for example, the policy analyst should begin by reviewing recent trends and results of past efforts to provide jobs to welfare recipients. What worked? What did not? And why? Are more people joining welfare roles or are people staying on welfare for longer periods? The former may imply quite different causal factors than the latter—a temporary economic slowdown versus a permanent decline in the ability of unskilled people to find work (Leahy, Buss, & Quane, 1996).

As well as providing perspective and sharpening analysis, knowing what has been tried may point to potential political problems and may identify important words and concepts to be used when communicating with decision makers. Resurrecting diagnoses and prescriptions used previously to little effect will attract few decision makers. The policy analyst must differentiate new rhetoric and proposals. This isn't easy. In academe, careers are made by repackaging tattered ideas. Likewise, in policy circles the same ideas resurface time after time—the dolphin effect. The Johnson administration's war on poverty, Bush's community empowerment, and Clinton's empowerment zones are strikingly similar (Rubin, 1994).

But don't be trapped by historical analogies. Examine apparent similarities between today's problems and those of the past. For example, it may be tempting to view the need to train today's unemployed people as analogous to the conditions after World War II when millions of discharged soldiers threatened to flood the labor market. In 1946, Congress reacted by creating the GI Bill. Would that work today? Perhaps. But GI Bill participants were mature and motivated; many untrained people in the workforce today are not.

Richard Neustadt and Ernest May (1986), authors of *Thinking in Time,* offer rules to reduce the chances of being misled by history: "Ask, what's the story? How did these concerns develop? Remember that issues for decision makers are concerns appropriate to them, derived from their presumptions (or yours on their behalf) in the face of the knowns and uncertainties before them. Construct timelines. Start the story as far back as it properly goes and plot trends while entering signal events, especially big changes. Don't foreshorten the history in ways that distort it. Don't neglect political changes" (Neustadt & May, 1986, p. 235).

The essential matter of history is not what happened but what people thought or said about it. To be useful, therefore, a policy history must include political history. Who supported previous education reforms? How did the town react when the state changed waste disposal laws? What position did the local chapter of the American Association of Retired People (AARP) take on banking reforms? Tracing political history is difficult. It's easy to find out what happened; it's difficult to find out who pushed and pulled behind the scenes, or why. But exploring an issue's history helps us think through where we are, where we are going, and how to get there.

SUMMARY

Policy problems are characterized by information in the political arena. Not all information is created equal. Some is patently false, yet widely believed to be true. Alternatively, some is true, yet everywhere treated as false. Some is half true. Some is distorted. Much is highly subjective. Policy analysts must sift through facts and figures, looking for credible information on which to base their problem assessment. Just as it is dangerous for physicians to jump to conclusions about illnesses, so too must policy analysts keep an open mind. But also like physicians, policy analysts should be skeptical, but not cynical, about information, always evaluating its reliability. Policy analysts must always ask: who, what, when, where, why, and how. Who benefits, who loses? Policy analysts must focus intensely on the history of issues, just as physicians review patient histories. A historical review not only frames the issue but offers clues as to how different frameworks might be constructed to solve problems.

CASE STUDIES

"A problem well stated," someone said, "is a problem half-solved." So the policy analyst must find accurate descriptions of social problems. Easier said than done.

Caseloads from scores of public and private social welfare agencies are important sources of data for defining the nature and extent of social problems. Important, but not always reliable. Agencies know their funding may depend on caseloads. To inflate client numbers, some resort to "cooking the books" (see Stockman, 1983). Therefore, treat caseload data with care: Check it before you use it.

In 1977, Youngstown suffered the first of a wave of massive plant closings (Buss & Redburn, 1983). Uncertain what services displaced workers would need, state and local officials relied on reported caseloads. Because agencies protect client privacy, few analysts know how caseload data are gathered, analyzed, packaged, and interpreted before they are publicly released. Agencies are not necessarily deliberately deceiving analysts or policymakers. Social data are complex and easily misinterpreted. But analysts should note Victor Hugo's maxim: "Ministers say what one wants them to say so that one may do what they want one to do."

In 1985, university researchers studied monthly, quarterly, and annual caseload data of 30 agencies in 10 counties over a 10-year period. Their findings do not necessarily apply to reporting practices in all states or communities, but they reveal the dangers of relying on agency reports (Buss & Vaughan, 1988).

Case A. A Community Mental Health Center. One mental health agency received extra funding by reporting increases in the numbers of displaced workers seeking services. But researchers found that the agency counted as clients not only displaced workers but their family members as well—even when they were not in the labor force and had not lost jobs.

Case B. Psychiatric Hospitals. Caseloads in hospitals shift not only as a result of changes in patient numbers but also as a result of changes in how long patients are kept in the facility. If the number of patients seeking help fell, researchers found, hospitals prolonged the average patient stay. As the number of patients increased, they stayed for shorter periods.

Case C. Police Crime Statistics. Comparing crime rates among jurisdictions is difficult because—except for the seven index crimes reported to the FBI—different police departments report data differently. Some cities treat offenders as cases (so five charges filed against an offender counts as one case). Others treat charges against offenders as separate cases. Arrests are also not treated consistently. The number of cases reported by a police department is also related to the size of the police force: the more officers, the more cases.

Case D. Children's Services. Child abuse is an important indicator of need for children's services. Yet, care is needed in interpreting agency reports of child abuse. In Youngstown, all agencies reported a dramatic increase in "reports of child abuse." But these reports refer to any contact with the agency concerning child abuse. Substantiated cases of child abuse actually declined.

Case E. Alcoholism Treatment Centers. Centers in Youngstown reported a sharp increase in caseloads after plant closings, usually winning extra funding to help them cope with the consequences. But researchers found the caseload increased precipitously just after the closing as a result of changes in the definition of a case. Under the new rules, anyone entering the agency's door was a case, even if he or she never participated in any programs. The old definition required a "case" to visit the agency at least three times. The apparent increase in cases following the closing was simply people completing required visits to be counted as cases: three visits counted as one case, then one case expanded into three based on visits. There was no real correlation between caseload and plant closing.

Case F. Employment Service Programs. The number of people receiving unemployment insurance benefits, or the number of new claims during a month, are widely used indicators of the local economy. In Youngstown, one employment service (ES) office reported that its caseload had risen by 10,000 as a result of the plant closing. Researchers found that the actual number was one half the estimate by the ES. The ES office had counted laid-off workers temporarily recalled and then laid off again as two cases.

Case G. Welfare Expenditures. Welfare budgets indicate local distress. Yet, comparisons among counties can be misleading. In Youngstown, some county offices supported nursing homes from the welfare budget; others did not. Some reported capital costs for nursing homes as a human service expenditure; others reported them under an entirely separate line item.

3

Diagnosing

*Unlike the faith-healer, whose cures are believed to be
comprehensively beneficial, the expert healer . . . must identify
what he is dealing with: he must size up the situation, distinguish
one illness from another and recognize what its susceptibilities are
likely to be. He looks for causes and tries to treat them. But before
looking for causes, he must have a list of relevant possibilities in
mind. All medical inquiries take place within a more or less
circumscribed domain of theoretical commitment in which
curiosity is limited by what the investigator regards as possible.
Within the range of what is possible he arranges alternatives in
order of their probability. Investigation presupposes suspicion.*

Jonathan Miller, *The Body in Question* (1978, p. 2)

Diagnosis is tough. Patients demand alleviation of symptoms and may
self-diagnose to speed treatment. The complexity of economic and
social maladies tempts decision makers to direct programs at symptoms,
not causes. Because symptoms are clearly visible, plausible treatments
are easy to devise. Enroll those who lost their jobs in retraining. Require
low-scoring school children to take extra science and math. Offer public
loans to small businesses denied credit by banks. Provide federal grants
to repair potholes in roads. Mandate work when welfare caseloads grow.

Decision makers leap from describing symptoms to prescription without
diagnosing causes. Treating symptoms rarely solves policy problems—any
more than prescribing analgesics cures gravely ill patients. Displaced workers are trained in skills for which trainers have spare instructors, not necessarily in skills needed by local employers. Following massive, permanent
layoffs in the steel industry in Youngstown, for example, the federal Training
Adjustment Act program mostly funded training programs to allow displaced
workers to complete apprenticeships in steelmaking, where labor surpluses
existed. Enforced extra study raises dropout rates among local students,
improving performance rates on proficiency tests because the dropouts do not

take the tests. Small business loan subsidies waste money, either providing capital to those who do not need it or offering capital to those who should not have it (Vaughan et al., 1984). Local highway administrators allow good roads to deteriorate to claim more pothole money from federal government. And people on welfare may be ill suited for work, lacking skills, motivation, support resources, or capacity.

But effective treatments addressing root causes are more difficult to devise than focusing on signs and symptoms. In medicine, physicians employ procedures to help them arrive at accurate diagnoses before proceeding to prescription. Policy analysts must follow similar protocols: (a) suggest several possible hypotheses consistent with symptoms; (b) examine evidence to determine whether one hypothesis offers the most likely explanation, while at the same time rejecting for good reason as many competing hypotheses as possible; and (c) assemble evidence to defend that diagnosis to patients and public.

Diagnosis, therefore, is based on formulating alternative explanations—not on a rush to reach a single conclusion (Lasswell, 1971; Stinchcombe, 1968). Competing hypotheses must be consistent with observed symptoms and logically plausible. Evaluating hypotheses may be costly and, more important, time consuming. The policy analyst's art strikes a balance between testing all possible hypotheses and accepting the first plausible diagnosis. The first approach leads to fewer errors but may not be complete until the patient dies or walks unaided out of the emergency room. The second approach is faster but more prone to error. Ironically, physicians face the same issues: Rushing to judgment is called the *cascade effect* in medicine.

To restore a patient to health, or at least to alleviate suffering, physicians need to answer at least six questions about the patient's condition:

1. Is the disease congenital, that is, was the patient born with it? Or did he or she contract it?

2. If the condition is congenital, was the patient born with the illness or with an anomaly creating a predisposition toward some illness (the child of a diabetic, for example, may not be born with diabetes but with a predisposition to contracting it later in life)?

3. Is the condition acute or chronic?

4. If the condition is acute, will the patient's own immune system or defense mechanisms, aided by medical intervention, bring about a full recovery?

5. If the condition is chronic, is a full recovery possible or will the patient continue to deteriorate?

6. If the patient recovers, will he or she be left with a predisposition toward contracting the illness again?

Policy analysts sometimes fail to go through an analogous checklist when they begin diagnostics. Answering these questions can help. Consider the case of discouraged workers (Buss & Redburn, 1986; see also, "The Overlooked Housekeeper," 1994). In the 1980s, government decision makers were driven to address the discouraged worker problem—armies of displaced workers dropping out of the labor force because they could not find jobs. The problem of discouragement was misdiagnosed because the decision makers failed to look more closely at who discouraged workers really are. To be considered discouraged by the U.S. Bureau of Labor Statistics (BLS), persons must be adults not working, having not looked for work, and having given up looking for work because they believe that they are not qualified for available work or that no jobs are available. Without considering the BLS definition and research underlying it, the proper diagnosis would be need for retraining and job placement assistance.

A closer look at discouraged workers would have revealed a different diagnosis altogether (Buss & Redburn, 1986). Discouraged workers are primarily people who have never worked and only intend to work under highly limited circumstances—restricted hours, specific salaries, and certain jobs. In other words, they are not displaced or unemployed workers down on their luck, they are people only weakly attached to the labor force. A retraining and job placement program would be of little help for and of little interest to most discouraged workers.

In this chapter, we offer rules for formulating and evaluating alternative diagnoses.

RULE 1: DEVELOP COMPETING HYPOTHESES

Deriving competing hypotheses explaining, rather than simply describing a problem, is the most difficult part of the diagnostic art. Explanation offers a plausible reason for observed behavior—pushing behind the surface of an issue to create a convincing story. For example, a popular explanation for rising malpractice insurance costs in the mid-1980s was soaring damage awards. But this begs the question of why juries across the country suddenly began awarding high damages. The lemming instinct is rarely a satisfactory answer. Reasoning further that falling inflation may have cut insurance company earnings, forcing them to raise premiums, may explain the problem's timing more fully. So, initial policy responses attempting to cap jury awards were ill founded.

Formulating diagnoses can be approached systematically by posing two questions:

1. Does the problem result from private or public actions? The distinction between private and public actions is vital because private and public people and institutions face different behavioral incentives and their actions must be explained differently. Policies to deal with problems originating in public agency initiatives will probably be very different from those to deal with the consequences of private actions.

2. Is the problem systemic or nonsystemic? If the problem is systemic—that is, recurrent or widespread—appropriate treatment may be to change how decisions reduce harmful consequences. If the problem stems from consequences of an isolated act, then the issue may deal with consequences of events rather than preventing or reversing their occurrences.

Both dimensions above fit neatly into a matrix for diagnosing policy problems—systemic and nonsystemic—arising from private or public actions:

	Public	*Private*
Systemic	welfare dependency; homelessness; inner city decline; tax incentives to business	environmental pollution; denial of credit to inner city borrowers
Nonsystemic	subsidizing professional sports arenas when not in public interest; dispersing housing subsidies to political chronies; campaign financing gimmicks	plant closings; insider trading on stock exchange; Medicaid/Medicare fraud

Policy issues like those in the cells in this matrix provide the basis for the rules immediately following.

RULE 2: DETERMINE WHETHER THE PROBLEM IS CAUSED BY PRIVATE ACTIONS

The actions of private institutions or people cause many problems. The opening of a large factory, for example, may stretch the capacity of the local water and sewer systems, schools, or highways. The closing of a large plant may leave thousands jobless. Waste disposal may jeopardize the health of nearby residents. Changing technologies may leave firms without appropriately trained personnel. But we must distinguish between an event resulting from private actions and a problem redolent of public agencies' inability to deal with that event (Squire & van der Tak, 1975; Ward & Deren, 1991).

In 1987, for example, state officials in Michigan created a rural strategy to address problems of the state's Upper Peninsula. Much of the 1980s dealt with critical industrial issues. Although urban areas recovered, unemployment in rural areas remained high. Many observers believed that the Upper Peninsula's dependence on resource-based industries caused problems. This diagnosis was about 10 years out of date.

A detailed study of the region's economy, completed in 1989, found that unemployment fell rapidly after 1985 (Buss & Gemmel, 1994). Although economic expansion in the 1970s depended almost entirely on pulp and paper and iron ore industries, job growth in the late 1980s occurred across many industries and was slow in these traditional resource industries. In fact, workforces in traditional companies shrank as employers introduced labor-saving machinery and production methods. A rushed diagnosis could have led to a strategy to support resource-based industries at a time when they were dramatically restructuring.

Private actions often reveal problems in state and local government policies by subjecting them to stress. A plant closing, for example, may represent the job service's inability to cope with a sudden surge of new claimants. New residential development may overload sewers or overcrowd schools. To the extent that any problem is ultimately treated by a new public initiative, we have implicitly diagnosed its cause—at least in part—as a problem of the government's role in shaping development: Perhaps, the wrong rules for guiding private action were enacted, the wrong rules were enforced, or programs were poorly designed.

Systemic Problems Arising
From Private Actions

Systemic problems arise when private actions by different actors repeatedly lead to similar problems. Examples include the pollution of lakes and rivers, brokers trading on inside information, and banks refusing credit to small businesses or inner-city borrowers. There are three reasons why private parties may act this way.

First, rules may not require private entities to consider the consequences of their actions. Polluters, for example, may not be required to consider the consequences to other users of water or to its natural habitants of discharging wastes. Problems falling into this category include *externalities* (Amacher & Ulbrich, 1986; Musgrave & Musgrave, 1990), as well as cases where values exhibited by private parties clash with values adopted by the government. For example, employers who systematically refused to hire members of racial minorities (before the enactment of the Equal Rights Amendment) were not breaking the law but were causing a systemic problem requiring public action.

Externalities conceal or distort valuable information from decision makers. They also distort incentives. Automobile drivers are only dimly aware that each mile traveled imposes costs on others, but have no way of estimating how great these costs might be or any incentives to reduce them. Public action may bring about a more efficient, and even more equitable solution, although not in every case. User fees or tolls on highways are examples.

Examples of externalities are

- *Environmental spillovers,* such as fish killed in a public stream by fertilizer runoff from a farmer's land, odor downwind of a power plant, or pollution of groundwater by heavy metals from mine tailings;

- *Aesthetic benefits (or costs)* people would pay for (or to avoid), such as the view offered by an urban park (or an unsightly lot filled with abandoned automobiles);

- *Common property problems,* such as several farmers tapping into the same aquifer, increasing costs of fellow users by drawing down the water table, or rush-hour commuters whose automobiles cause traffic congestion;

- *Physical or cultural amenities,* such as museums or theaters, contributing to people's sense of well-being even if they do not use them. Some people value big-city ambiance or rural access even if they do not use them.

What these externalities have in common is that important decisions are made—application of fertilizer, abandonment of an automobile, pumping from an aquifer, or building of a museum—while excluding some people affected by, and prepared to pay to influence, outcomes. People wanting to fish in the polluted stream could pay farmers to reduce fertilizer use, but no forum to allocate stream usage among competitors exists, save perhaps the courts.

Problem categorization or assessment is itself problematic. For example, plant closings may appear similar to water pollution—a widespread problem imposing heavy costs on unwitting third parties. Several states followed this diagnosis and enacted legislation requiring advance notification and even payment of reemployment costs by companies closing plants.

The analogy is inappropriate, however. Pollutors do not consider water pollution costs (unless forced by law enforcement to do so), but the value of jobs terminated in a plant closing have been weighed by those shutting down. The *social costs* associated with closings have not been ignored (Coase, 1960). The value of what these workers produce is less than the costs of producing it. Workers lost buyers for their products. This should not be diagnosed as an externality. Some people argue that plant owners are shortsighted, but they rarely explain why. There may be aspects of the tax system or results of state regulations that discourage farsighted private management. If policies cause problems, diagnosis should analyze them.

The second reason why private actions may systematically create problems that enter the public sphere is that laws are broken. Dumping toxic waste in deserted areas or waterways, for example, should not be treated as an externality—dumpers know the costs of their actions. Necessary environmental laws were in place but not strictly enforced. Similarly, the wave of insider-trading cases on Wall Street in 1987 did not reflect the failure of capital markets or absence of appropriate laws as much as the failure to adequately regulate. A diagnosis should try to determine whether systematic violation of laws indicates that penalties are too small relative to the advantages of illegal actions (many people regard a parking fine as a cheap alternative to parking garages) or because the probability of being caught is very small (as it is for many forms of tax evasion).

The third reason why private actions may cause systemic problems is through the *unintended consequences* of public actions. For example, banks may not be willing to extend credit to small and new businesses because they operate in markets protected by state regulations that restrict new entrants and therefore feel no competitive pressure to serve marginal customers. Bank regulation also requires bankers to follow "prudent person" criteria in investing to protect corporate shareholders.

In all three cases, the appropriate response involves policies to change private decision-making processes—requiring externalities to be *internalized* (costs of externalities included in price), the law to be obeyed, or public incentives to be redirected. This can only be done effectively if we have accurately identified the policymakers, decisions, and determinants causing the problem.

Nonsystemic Problems Arising
From Private Actions

Problems can arise from large-scale private actions—opening or closing a private enterprise, large relative to the community in which it is located, precipitates economic and social problems. Sudden increases in energy prices in 1973 and 1979 also created profound adjustment problems. In most instances, remedial policies focus on helping people and institutions adjust to the consequences, although policies may include measures to slow down impacts to provide people with "breathing room." A useful problem diagnosis should involve impact projections of private action.

Predicting consequences of an event as devastating and as complex as a plant closing or the sudden increase in energy prices are difficult but not beyond reach. At such times, we seek historical analogies or examples from other states for clues. But analogies must be chosen with care (McCloskey, 1985b; Neustadt & May, 1986).

The confusing national response to the sudden energy price increases during the 1970s also reflect adoption of the wrong analogy. President Carter did not label the energy crisis "the moral equivalent of war" until 1979, but Congress viewed OPEC's actions as warlike and energy policy as analogous to wartime mobilization from 1974. Yet, the purpose of wartime mobilization policy is, in part, to protect people from the consequences of temporarily shifting resources from peacetime to military activity through price controls and rationing. Oil today remains at several times its 1973 price and it is clear that the problem in 1973 was to help people adjust to higher prices rather than to shield them.

Even if data are assembled, they mislead if used in the wrong model. An econometric study pushed Congress toward adopting its approach to energy policy. This study purported to prove that the public would not cut consumption in response to higher energy prices, which drive up imports, weaken the dollar, and leave the nation vulnerable to future boycotts. The study analyzed relationships between changes in gasoline purchases and fluctuations of oil prices after World War II—a period during which there had been a strong secular downward trend in oil prices with small, short-term fluctuations. Congress imposed the chaotic and enormously expensive federal allocation program although consumers exhibited a responsiveness to higher prices at least 10 times that originally estimated in the ill-fated study.

Decision makers often feel helpless in the face of a highly technical study describing statistical techniques in awe-inspiring detail. But no study is better than the data and assumptions shaping it, and a conclusion defying common sense and past experience should be challenged. Historical analogies of consumer responsiveness to price increases abound—only a century ago the growing shortage of whale oil precipitated the search for alternatives leading to the discovery of petroleum in Pennsylvania and to changes in work patterns in making fuller use of daylight.

RULE 3: DETERMINE WHETHER THE PROBLEM IS CAUSED BY GOVERNMENT INTERVENTION

It is common for professional economists when they first come into contact with administrators, to feel that the administrator is grossly ignorant of elementary economics. Sometimes this is justified; but it is equally true that the professional economist may be grossly ignorant of administration.
—Sir Alec Cairncross, *Essays in Economic Management* (1971, p. 66)

A lot of problems today directly result from government intervention. Government activities touch most aspects of economic and social life—tax codes influence investments, state management of education shapes investments in human capital, and capital spending programs determine the condition of infrastructure. Today's systemic problems are often caused—directly or indirectly—by government actions. Nonsystemic problems result from poor administration, possibly reflecting on the diligence with which executive staff oversee work of appointed administrators, and from corruption.

**Systemic Problems Resulting
From Public Actions**

Systematic problem symptoms characteristic of a government program include the public perception that service is not offered equitably—the program may be failing to serve people perceived as deserving or discriminating in a way lacking public support, or the program may be performing poorly relative to similar services in other states or services offered privately, or it may create bottlenecks in private activities—protracted permitting or hearing processes, for example.

Diagnosis should check five aspects of program management:

1. What evidence measures the program's performance? Regular management information is vital to program success.
2. Does the program have feasible, internally consistent goals, and are these goals understood by administrative staff?
3. Do the consequences of good and bad performance reinforce basic program objectives?

4. Do program managers enjoy the discretionary flexibility to get the most from available resources?

5. Is the program adequately funded?

But even this practice can be problematic. In 1995, the National Academy of Public Administration, under contract with the Advisory Council on Intergovernmental Relations (ACIR, 1996), conducted a nationwide survey of state agencies responsible for infrastructure—highways, waste treatment, and the like—to document the best practices in benchmarking. The researchers discovered that most agencies had in place elaborate systems for setting goals and objectives against standards incorporating policies like those in profit-making organizations. But performance in the agencies was not rewarded or penalized in budgets or promotions, and agency clients had no input into the process. In short, the agencies developed measures and gathered performance data but did not use it.

These questions must be answered as part of public policy evaluation. Chapter 6 discusses programs and techniques for measuring outcomes in detail.

Nonsystemic Problems Resulting From Public Actions

Nonsystemic problems are less frequent than systemic problems, or so we hope, but they can be devastating. The malfeasance of one appointed official or one careless act—painfully revealed in the press—can outweigh many person-hours of good government practiced by other administrators. A diagnosis may become an autopsy. Problems of this dimension are rightfully translated by the public as a sign of poor executive management—why wasn't the problem caught at an earlier stage?

Residents of Washington, D.C., will recall the ill-fated decision of the city council in summer 1996 to cut funding of city offices across the board to avoid certain default. Unfortunately, funding to the coroner's office was suspended as well, causing the coroner to stack unautopsied corpses in hallways, having run out of refrigerator storage space. Among other things, lack of forensics stifled many a murder investigation during the period.

Not all nonsystemic problems can be caught, but more can be done. The most powerful diagnostic tool for nonsystemic as well as for systemic problems is regular program performance monitoring, such as *accountability meetings* between the chief executive and his or her staff and administrators to discuss objectives, problems, and performance.

RULE 4: ANALYZE HYPOTHESES

The policy analyst should emerge from the first step of diagnosis with two or three possible explanations for a problem to which one or two hypotheses may be added because they are widely ascribed to executive or legislative leadership. The process may seem protracted compared with that described previously. But it does not have to be. For many issues, diagnostics may be conducted on the back of an envelope. The flagship urban program, the Urban Development Action Grant (UDAG), was developed on the back of a napkin by high-level presidential nominees. But lack of time or reliable numbers does not invalidate the overall process. The diagnostic process prevents us from rushing to judgment. It ensures that we fact-check—if only through tough questioning of people involved. It also ensures that we explore the issue's history—again, this may be no more than questioning knowledgeable people. Most important, it demands we try to develop more than one plausible problem explanation.

The unwillingness of local banks to lend to small businesses might, for example, elicit three hypotheses: (a) that the problem lay in the failure of the potential borrowers to prepare convincing business plans, (b) that the banking community was complacent and unwilling to make difficult loans, and (c) that there was insufficient competition among lenders because of state (or federal) banking regulations.

Analysis of the mediocre quality of primary and secondary education may have yielded more hypotheses: poorly qualified teachers, outdated curriculum, lack of parental involvement, overly bureaucratic school districts, poor links to the world of work, or the absence of kindergarten to prepare children, for example.

Testing involves finding out more about the issue (have these hypotheses been researched before?) and exploring their logical consistency (what other economic phenomena does each hypothesis imply?). The goal is not to arrive at a single acceptable hypothesis—many explanations abound—but to arrive at a ranking of different explanations according to their likelihood and importance. For some issues, explanations may only be determined by the experimental application of different remedies. For these issues, treatments will be applied as *pilot* projects, with the relative effectiveness of different pilots indicating the relative importance of different explanations. Why welfare caseloads are increasing, for example, might be tested by initiating several experimental programs—an employer wage subsidy, a counseling and job search assistance program, a public employment project, and a supported work program. A program to encourage displaced workers to start their own businesses might allow people to receive their unemployment insurance check in a lump sum to capitalize a new business. Their relative effectiveness might indicate the relative importance of work barriers facing low-income people and thus guide future funding allocations.

RULE 5: FOLLOW UP ON THE DIAGNOSIS

Diagnoses must be checked. Physicians recognize that the patient's health is so complicated and important, and the application of the wrong treatment can be so costly and dangerous, that their original diagnosis should be revisited after treatment begins. The policy analyst's hurried environment often means an issue will only be reexamined if the problem worsens or if the treatment exhibits serious side effects. Since all diagnoses are provisional, analysts must always find ways of finding out if they were right. This need not require lengthy evaluation. An informal callback to the agency charged with solving the problem, a meeting of relevant parties, monitoring economic statistics, or conducting an elementary test can correct problems quickly, without too much media attention.

What are the barriers to self-healing? As in medicine, or perhaps even more so, most problems eventually solve themselves. People move away from declining communities, businesses move in, and schools improve. But how quickly will self-correcting mechanisms come into play? Who will be left behind? Decision makers must try to set priorities by picking issues that have the greatest difficulty for resolution.

Failure of a rural community to recover from a shock may reflect a lack of capacity to deal collectively with issues. People may be deeply divided about growth—some wanting to expand by attracting "big box" stores like Wal-Mart, others wanting to preserve the local quality of life in farmlands and wooded areas. Conflicts in values are present in all public decision making. What some communities lack is knowledge of how to resolve conflicts. Conflict resolution is *not* a process of achieving *consensus*—growth and no-growth or right-to-life and pro-choice advocates will likely never agree. *Conflict resolution* is the art of achieving *compromise*. It is often the least glamorous, but most important, part of dealing with rural development problems and others.

Issues tending not to improve over time have some of the following characteristics:

- *Require complex and profound adjustments mixing public and private responses*—for example, tax and regulatory changes, acquisition of new skills and new technologies needed to allow a competitive telecommunications industry to emerge

- *Show little sign of abating over 2 or 3 years*—Youngstown, Ohio, for example, experienced little relative change in its economic distress for at least 8 years following the first plant closing

- *Require a solution that is blocked by federal policies and programs*—for example, full recovery of agricultural communities may require further changes in federal policies

- *Are managed by interest groups more powerful than policy-makers*—for example, failure to reform Social Security and the power of the aging lobby

- *Are bad economics*—for example, subsidizing firms to locate in distressed communities (see Ladd, 1994)

SUMMARY

Once policy analysts, and their physician counterparts, clearly understand the signs and symptoms, they begin to offer hypotheses explaining the problem from various perspectives. In psychiatry, for example, a psychological problem may be diagnosed as resulting from trauma, learned behavior, chemical imbalances, psychosomatic disorder, or neurosis or psychosis. In policy analysis, analysts look to see whether the problem emanates from public or private actions and from systemic factors or individual actions as a way of narrowing down causes. Once competing hypotheses have been laid out, data and information are brought to bear to eliminate unlikely hypotheses until one or two remain. After diagnosing, policy analysts continually follow up. Social science policy research, if well done, can greatly inform the process of eliminating competing hypotheses.

CASE STUDY

Diagnosis is not intuitively obvious. To illustrate how we can use the process, consider an example. In 1988, a western state was concerned that the shrinking oil business, coupled with a slump in ranching, threatened its rural development. New business birth rates were far below the region's average, and the share of new businesses that became high-growth enter-prises was among the nation's lowest.

Step 1. Define the real problem. We must first sort out the real nature of the problem. Are things as bad as they seem? Is the problem described in different ways in different regions of the state? By different interest groups? What empirical evidence supports anecdotal evidence? A re-view of several sources of data in the western state supported the original description of the problem. The state suffered from a very low rate of new business starts—lower than would be expected given other studies of rural entrepreneurship conducted by the Council of State Policy and Planning Agencies (Lin, Buss, & Popovich, 1990).

Step 2. Develop alternative hypotheses, consistent with symptoms, that could explain the problem as resulting from private or public actions. Once we are confident about a problem's characterization, we seek explanations for its occurrence. First, we ask whether the problem is systemic. By reviewing the history of new business starts, we may conclude that the state suffered from a low rate of business formation for a long time and in all regions. The problem does not appear to result from recent downturns in oil and gas activity. It appears to be systemic.

Different parties offered hypotheses. From interviews with entrepre-neurs, we know that local banks are unwilling to lend to new businesses. But from interviews with local banks, we learn that they fund all viable commercial and industrial projects, and that those refused loans are "not bankable." We thus have two competing hypotheses. We must develop ways to test them. This means collecting further data. We have two sources—people who have been refused loans, and bankers who have refused them. Neither may be as objective as we wish.

From a survey of recent new business starters, we learn that a large number were financed by out-of-state banks after being refused credit from local banks. This is not consistent with the view that local banks make all viable business loans. From a review of federal banking data, we discover that local banks hold a smaller share of their assets in commercial and industrial loans than do the banks in neighboring states. They also report a much lower default rate on commercial and industrial loans than do banks in neighboring states. They appear less willing to take risks than banks in neighboring states. Although the evidence can never *prove* one hypothesis correct, it may be consistent with one hypothesis rather than another. In this case, the evidence is more consistent with the hypothesis that low busi-ness formation rates relate to the unwillingness of bankers to make loans.

But our diagnosis should not stop here. An explanation of a problem that depends on behavioral tendencies is rarely satisfactory. Why are local bankers so averse to risks? Why haven't more entrepreneurial banks moved in to serve? Comparing state bank regulations with those in adjacent states may provide hypotheses. We find that our state prohibits branch banking and limits the ability of out-of-state banks to move in. This may provide local bankers with a protected monopoly. Other banks cannot open competing branches in the community. As the economist Alfred Marshall observed, the most popular way in which monopoly rents are taken is through a quiet life (Heyne, 1973, p. 155). For bankers, a quiet life means not getting involved in marginal loans.

Step 3. Can we defend our diagnosis against alternative hypotheses? We are confident that we have reached the right diagnosis. But we must press on. We must make sure that we can defend our diagnosis against alternative explanations. If we plan to encourage greater banking competition, we can trust local bankers to lobby fiercely against it. Diagnoses must not only be right—they must be defensible.

4

Prescribing

*. . . medicine seeks to palliate, find acceptable compromises,
ways of buying time. It seeks to prolong life rather than cure
a disease once and for all. Perhaps the term "art of healing"
is too ambitious and we should substitute "art of helping."
The only true cure would mean eliminating death.
Medicine proposes to hold death off as long as possible
and is not terribly fussy about how it is done.*

—Lucien Israel, MD,
Decision-Making: The Modern Doctor's Dilemma (1982, p. 10)

For most medical conditions, diagnosis determines treatment or signifi-
cantly reduces treatment options. A broken limb must be immobilized,
a bacterial infection treated with antibiotics, an open wound sutured.
For other conditions, physicians must weigh desired treatment outcomes against possible adverse therapeutic side effects. Treating
asthma, arthritis, or dermatitis with hormonal preparations offers patients immediate, almost miraculous, relief from symptoms, but long-
term side effects may be devastating—including disruption of the
hormonal system, upset metabolism, and even disturbed functioning of
the skeletal system. Arriving at the best *trade-off* between immediate
relief and long-term damage requires physicians to consult closely with
the patient.

Most policy interventions more closely resemble the second medical
treatment than the first. There are almost always adverse side effects—
someone must pay for the program or someone loses preferential treatment
from a change in regulations. Do deteriorating roads need more spending,
a change in priorities, exclusion of heavy trucks from some roadways, or
a study commission? Should we act today or next year when the fiscal
picture may have improved? If we must spend more money, where do we
get it? Treatment choice is extensive and uncertainty surrounding the
consequences of each choice is humbling.

Neither physicians nor policy analysts can easily—in many cases—prove the efficacy of all their treatments. Causal links between intervention and outcome are often tenuous. Think of the debate in the medical community over the efficacy of vitamins, exercise, angioplasty, low-fat diets, and other basic health practices. But decision makers often know much less about how well their policy treatments work than do physicians.

Uncertainty discourages innovation. Experiments risk patients' health as well as practitioners' reputations, not to mention lawsuits. They create fads in treatment. Do what everyone else is doing and you can receive some professional or political protection—"We followed standard procedures" or "We are doing what our competitor states are doing." So, many state and local governments start up new programs with no more motivation than that their neighbors created similar initiatives—the policy analog of defensive medicine.

Problems and policies that often appear analogous on the surface turn out not to be so on deeper examination. Most stories of successful programs or policies from other communities are merely widely publicized tips of policy icebergs. Below the waterline are many similar programs that failed elsewhere. For example, states concerned with setting up a state agency to fund new products looked only at the Connecticut Product Development Corporation—which managed, after 5 years, to cover costs—and ignored the score of similar programs in other states that were losing money with little hope of ever breaking even. Any state starting a program for financing development of new products today might have a 1 in 20 chance of earning a rate of return equal to or above what it could have earned investing in a safe money market account. A community bank, the success of which depended on the energy and skills of its founder, is cloned to serve a multitude of poor neighborhoods. But the clones lack similar energy, competence, commitment, or ability. Clones almost always disappoint. To avoid this, policy analysts should scrutinize overall success rates of a proposed approach and not be dazzled by shining examples.

But although physicians can turn to detailed laboratory studies, summarized in comprehensive directories, reliable policy evaluations are rare. A series of U.S. General Accounting Office (GAO) assessments of federal programs in the 1990s illustrate the paucity of sound evaluation. GAO found few evaluation studies of programs in economic development (1996b), community development (1996a), small business development (1994c), education (1998), regional development such as the Tennessee Valley Authority (1996b), and training and retraining (1994a, 1994b), to name a few.

Few policymakers are eager to bestow the legacy of what they have learned from failures on future generations. This ironically parallels the

---

BOX 4.1

Boxes and Best Practices

Policy analysts should beware of two common practices in policy studies—use of policy **boxes** and **best practices**. Policy issue papers develop arguments favoring or opposing alternative courses of action. To illustrate points throughout without elaborate explanation, analysts resort to boxes—literally—in which thumbnail sketches of programs, projects, or policies are described, usually in one-half page or less. Our experience suggests that these boxes can oversimplify and oversell their referents because the lion's share have not been properly evaluated. Policymakers or analysts from other jurisdictions read the boxes, believe in their veracity, and adopt them as their own, often to see them fail.

Best practices are papers that purport to have reviewed policies, programs, or projects across the country, lighting on those representing the most successful or effective. Like their "boxed" counterparts above, best practices many times are public relations summaries of activities, not scientific evaluations. Again, policymakers adopting unexamined activities may be disappointed in their performance.

---

social science research enterprise. Failure to achieve desired results goes unreported in professional journals (Pedhazur & Schmelkin, 1991). What is reported does not reflect how the research was actually done—the context of discovery, versus the context of explanation. Perhaps the most valuable knowledge of all—failures—is lost. Even if a program has performed well elsewhere, similar success cannot be guaranteed at home because it may be implemented under very different circumstances.

Instead of the mechanistic application of cost-benefit techniques, the policy analyst might borrow the physician's approach. Physicians have the advantage of standard books not only describing drugs or therapies to cure different medical conditions but also laying out potential side effects. The Hungarian-born economist Janos Kornai (1983), exploring the link between medical practices and economic policy-making, was given a copy of *Meyler's Side Effects of Drugs—An Encyclopedia of Adverse Reactions*. "For me, an economist by profession, even the structure of the volume has been highly instructive," he writes.

It reviews the field by groups of medicaments and classifies the information with each group of medicaments according to the following subtitles:
(i) *Adverse reaction pattern.* The adverse side-effects are summed up here.
(ii) *Organs and systems.* This section examines in turn all parts, starting with the cardiovascular system and the respiratory system, through the

liver and kidney, and ending with the skin, and presents in detail all side-effects of the drug in question on these organs and systems.

(iii) *Risk situations.* The drug might, perhaps be given to a patient who, in addition to the disease for which the drug is intended, also suffers from another disease or from another anomaly, or with whom age (infant, child, aged) or pregnancy might cause additional problems. In considering the side-effects, particular attention has to be paid to these various risk situations.

(iv) *Interaction.* What is the effect of the drug in question if it is administered along with other drugs?

In connection with each statement, the book gives short information about the expected frequency of the side-effect and the sound foundations of the observation. It also raises such problems of side effects which have not yet been satisfactorily clarified, but also points to the necessity for further investigation. (p. 199)

As he turned the book's pages, Kornai felt "no small embarrassment in the name of my profession. How far we are from having systematically collected the adverse side-effects of therapies!" (p. 201). In the absence of analogous books for policy analysts and decision makers, we offer rules to help us identify competing policy interventions. Unlike the physician, the policy analyst should not offer only a single therapy. Remember that specification of alternatives underlies the power of the policy analyst's art.

What is the best way of selecting among alternatives? Policy analysts recommend techniques such as cost-benefit analysis. It offers, or so the claim goes, a useful set of rules for forecasting what will happen if alternative approaches are followed and how much they will cost. Cost-benefit analysis also offers basic rules for excluding certain outcomes from consideration (to avoid double counting) and for assigning those remaining outcomes into pro and con columns. The technique is briefly described in Chapter 6, "Evaluating." But it is not always easy to apply this framework because it may not incorporate many factors central to political decision makers, such as redistributional consequences and impacts of a decision on hard-to-measure aspects of our social and economic environment. The technique usually omits costs, risks, and benefits incurred in political decision making and fails to recognize that the political process is not risk-neutral.

RULE 1: SELECT THE APPROPRIATE BASELINE FOR DECISION MAKING

When cost-benefit analysis compares a policy response to a problem against doing nothing, costs usually overwhelm benefits. A tax increase is required, institutions must be closed, or user fees must be imposed. Analysis may have failed to project the full consequences of doing nothing. For example, the economic and political costs of raising water use charges to finance a wastewater treatment facility may be large enough to discourage starting the project. But these costs may shrink when compared with costs of a development moratorium imposed until the community complies with the Environmental Protection Agency's water quality standards. The costs of doing nothing are often unpaid for several years. As a result, decision makers overlook them. Almost all successful "investment" programs—prenatal care for low-income women, early childhood education programs, or education and training for juvenile offenders, for example—are frequent victims of budget cuts during recessions, even though they may be far more productive than programs offering more immediate benefits. The comparative baseline is not the present but a prediction of what is likely to happen in the future in the absence of any action. In some instances, inaction may worsen the problem—especially if actions offer very large benefits for a small cost per capita.

But inaction is often appropriate if natural "healing procedures" in the economy are likely to act faster than any government interventions. In these cases, it is easy to overemphasize the benefits of policies. There is usually a lag in collection and publication of economic data, for example. There is a further lag as data percolate into the public policy arena, another lag before performing diagnoses, yet another lag before taking action, and a final lag before actions exert influence. A study of federal countercyclical policies, for example, found the elapsed time from a cyclical downturn to the hiring of people under a public employment program ranged from 22 months to more than 4 years (Vaughan, 1980). Lags of this length yield more than enough time for cyclical problems to disappear.

An example of a problem that was rapidly abating even as states began to address it was the venture capital drought of the early 1980s. Statistics documented a shortage of equity capital for new ventures relative to the late 1960s just as other studies showed that new businesses accounted for over half of net new jobs. As a result, 28 states created venture capital corporations. As the legislation took effect, however, the problem was disappearing. In the first half of the 1970s, several events conspired to shrink the rate of investment in new ventures. As a result, the volume of new stock issues, a good measure of venture capital activity, fell from $1.3 billion in 1969 to $16 million in 1975. By 1982, most of the underlying causes of the venture capital shortage had been dealt with and there was strong evidence of a recovery in the venture capital market. But if policy analysts had simply examined the pattern of new capital and new placements in 1969 and in 1981, they would have gained a static picture of the venture capital market that indicated decline. Only by analyzing the dynamics of the market throughout the period could they have detected the strong turnaround in 1980. But only if they had identified the factors that had contributed to the shrinking of venture capital in the 1970s and had noted how those had changed could they have interpreted the latest statistics as a full recovery rather than as temporary "noise" and been able to project the results of taking no action accurately (see Vaughan et al., 1984).

RULE 2: ASSIGN PRIORITIES

Government decision makers, like physicians in medical centers, can be called on to address almost every problem concerning their constituents—from the aftermath of tornadoes and insect infestations to highway potholes and rising unemployment. No state or local government has the fiscal, executive, or legislative resources to meet all these demands, just as no emergency room can provide patients with all of the attention they demand. Even the federal government is humbled by the demands for action and a lack of resources to analyze them, much less make them right through policy interventions. Decision makers and physicians must determine what or who merits top priority.

Physicians can set priorities based on *triage*—who will survive anyway, who will die anyway, and who can benefit from medical attention (and for the jaundiced, who has health insurance and who does not), but setting policy priorities is much more political, depending on election promises, interest group pressures, the preferences of policymakers, and analysis of issues.

Once set, new priorities cannot easily jump the queue, however well chosen the policy and well reasoned its justification. Decision makers must familiarize themselves with the issues, weigh alternatives, and educate the public—both about problems and about options available for dealing with them. Even if a policy had a high probability of success, political credit for its enactment would be far less than for high-visibility issues attracting public attention. Priorities should influence how much attention accrues to different items and, perhaps, how risks are to be assessed.

Staff resources are almost always limited and must be focused on issues that are top priority in a decision maker's agenda, which usually involve large costs and benefits, are controversial, and are different from prior policies. No policy will score highly on all of these criteria. But the quality of decision making can be improved if issues are ranked on these considerations to determine how much staff time is to be spent on each.

RULE 3: WEIGH RELATIVE RISKS

Doctors must weigh *risks*. Medicine taken without fear by an otherwise healthy individual may be dangerous to a diabetic; an operation, routine for a young patient, may be catastrophic if carried out on an elderly patient. Decision makers often can be less cautious. They bravely propose favorite panaceas without considering whether economics or politics call for greater circumspection. Perhaps, they believe it possible to think up another curative intervention.

Yet, decision makers served by policy analysts often ask of them, "What guarantee do I have that this idea will work?" They are concerned with risk. Of course, there can be no guarantees in the world of public policy. But some actions represent much greater risks than others. The good analyst attempts to weigh risks associated with alternative policies.

Economists claim that risks can easily be included in the framework of cost-benefit analysis simply by weighing each outcome according to its probability. A cost with a 50% chance of occurring is simply discounted by half. This "objective" approach is useful in some instances. But it may conceal risks associated with the best and the worst possible outcomes. It also fails to allow for quite different weights associated with risk taking.

Decision makers' willingness to incur risks—their desire to avoid a large scale disaster or to go for a big payoff (economically and politically)— varies according to program priority, other types of policies pursued, public opinion, and the time in the election cycle. Decision makers may deal with low-priority issues with actions unlikely to cause serious damage but also unlikely to score large successes until they have studied the issue and educated the public. They may temporarily inject additional funds to preserve infrastructure while they review longer-term solutions and publicize needs for more expensive and painful solutions. Paradoxically, low-risk actions may include submission of radical legislation (without committing political capital to its passage) as a way of provoking debate without fearing the consequences of the bill's passage. For high-priority issues, after the public has been informed of options and their implications, the decision makers may be prepared to take risks.

If time permits, therefore, policy analysts should consider arraying choices in three different ways (see also, MacRae & Whittington, 1997):

(a) with no action as the baseline and outcomes weighted according to their summed probabilities; (b) laying out the least bad outcome for each choice—useful if decision makers are extremely cautious; and (c) arraying options according to their greatest minimum gain ("The least we can come away with is . . . "), useful when decision makers are willing to take risks to solve a problem.

RULE 4: CREATE A DIVERSIFIED POLICY PORTFOLIO

Interventions are part of a *portfolio* of actions taken to deal with political issues. Experienced politicians recognize this. That's why they often tackle difficult issues—the perennial unemployed inner-city youth, for example—with a flurry of demonstration projects intended to try several different approaches. And like any portfolio manager, a decision maker should be concerned not only about the risk of each policy considered separately but about interrelationships among the risks of different programs.

Failure to diversify can be costly. For example, state and local officials in Youngstown, Ohio, designed their development program to create a manufacturing industry to replace steel (Redburn & Buss, 1984). Their recruitment program, industrial parks, subsidized loans, and grants were all aimed at this goal. If one program failed, all were likely to fail, because all depended on the same economic view. States that place their faith in the job-creating power of a single new technology create similarly undiversified portfolios.

Correlating risk among policies can rarely be achieved statistically, but should be noted qualitatively. If an education reform package's success depends upon the administrative capacity of the state department of education, analysts should note that this is the case when calculating the risks for different initiatives.

RULE 5: DEFINE OPTIONS CLEARLY

Decision making—public and private, professional and personal—is an elusive process. In the political process, there is rarely a single decision maker. Decision making is a slow process of building consensus. Even an executive order—which the president or governor or mayor can issue unilaterally—emerges only after consultation with numerous stakeholders. To participate in this process, policy analysts must know the players, know the bureaucratic environment, and know the vocabulary. The political scientist John Kingdon (1986) describes the primeval idea soup from which policies grow:

> Generating alternatives and proposals resembles a process of biological natural selection. Much as molecules floated around in what biologists call the "primeval soup" before life came into being, so ideas float around in [the public policy] community. Many ideas are possible, much as many molecules would be possible. Ideas become prominent and then fade. There is a long process of "softening up": ideas are floated, bills introduced, speeches made; proposals are drafted, then amended in response to reaction and floated again. Ideas confront one another (much as molecules bump into one another) and combine with one another in various ways. The "soup" changes not only through the appearance of wholly new elements, but even more by the recombination of previously existing elements. While many ideas float around in this policy primeval soup, the ones that last, as in a natural selection system, meet some criteria. Some ideas thrive and prosper; some proposals are taken more seriously than others. (p. 52)

Policy analysis must assess the consequences of pursuing alternative policies. But policies are more than broad goals: Specific agencies or institutions carry them out. Social scientists are equipped to study how incentives influence human behavior and therefore to analyze how policies will affect and be affected by those charged with carrying them out. Although a policy may be appropriate for one agency—because of its powers, staff, and experience—it may be wholly inappropriate for another. Unless the policy analyst understands and takes bureaucratic context into account, analysis will be of little value. Economists refer to this as *agency effects.* Decision makers, immersed in details of public administration, may not even understand analysis that lacks a specific institutional context.

To influence public agency activity, social scientists must learn to think like practical decision makers. Rather than defining options in the absence of bureaucratic machinery, they must struggle to understand how policies and programs operate in context.

RULE 6: EXAMINE TODAY'S ACTIONS
AGAINST TOMORROW'S OPTIONS

In politics, no action is independent from other actions. Proposed policies cannot be examined in a vacuum. Every issue is tangled up with other issues. Building legislative and bureaucratic support for policies and programs is a complex trading process that ties up sizable amounts of political capital. Support for a new training initiative may require the governor or president to promise a new park in the district of an influential legislator who heads a key committee—*pork barrel* politics. The costs and benefits of a training program therefore include the costs and benefits of a recreation program—even though the link is political, not economic, and is certainly never presented in policy analysis.

Keeping options open is often attractive, particularly early in an administration or when there is little sense of how the problem will evolve or how policies will work. Some actions today shut off more future opportunities than others. Any program, once started, is difficult to stop. But conditional initiatives are easier to terminate or to modify if they fail to achieve provisional goals set for them (see below).

If comparing options today does not indicate a clearly preferable course of action, decision makers may want to delay until the severity of the problem is better understood or a favorable approach emerges. Therefore, the extent to which a policy maintains or narrows future options should be noted.

RULE 7: KNOW THE POLICY TIMETABLE

I took the draft bill in to the Senator—I was an eager young fellow at the time—and we engaged in pleasantries. After about twenty minutes, he indicated that I should leave. I said: "But Senator, don't you want to ask me any questions about this, discuss policy implications, or anything?" "No," he said, "I'll just introduce it tomorrow." Then he said, "Let me tell you something. We'll introduce it tomorrow but it will take twenty or twenty-five years for it to be brought into being. If it takes that long, there's not much point in my looking at the bill now, is there?"
—John Kingdon, *Congressmen's Voting Decisions* (1986, p. 72)

Legislation must be submitted before a certain date and last amendments must be introduced a few weeks later. Executive orders may have to be issued in time for the affected agencies to modify budget requests. Commissions and task forces must complete their work within a mandated time period. Analyses must be available before making decisions. Therefore, expert advice must be offered within an action timetable if it is to have any effect on outcomes. Sometimes, strong analyses can be introduced at any time, affecting the public's thinking about issues (e.g., medical reports on prescription drugs). But usually, information from experts must be introduced within the time horizons of busy elected officials. Figure 4.1 illustrates key stages in the *policy process* (Cook, 1993).

The issues tackled by decision makers change with the rhythms of election cycles. Decision making by governors or presidents is very different during the first year of a new term and during campaign months. A legislature acts on a different agenda during off years and during election years. A committee that has just wrestled to pass tax reform is unlikely to be interested in studies showing how to further refine the tax system. However convincing arguments for further reform, taxation is unlikely to return to the legislative agenda for some time. Analysts must be sensitive to these rhythms.

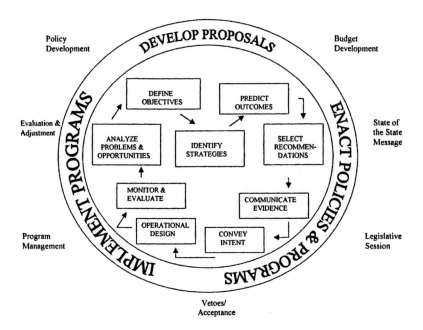

Figure 4.1. The Policy Cycle: State and Federal
SOURCE: Adapted from Cook (1993).

Issues also change as economic conditions and public perceptions change. The focus of policy analysis must adapt. The idea of a 5-cent-a-gallon increase in federal gas taxes had been around for a year before gloomy economic statistics in December 1982 allowed its passage as a jobs bill (Verdier, 1984, p. 426). Action-forcing events—such as a change in administration, a fiscal crisis, or a disaster—often create opportunities for thinking about problems in new ways. The policy consultant William Nothdurft (1988) argues, "A budget crisis is a liberating condition" (p. 2). When we cannot throw money at problems, we must innovate.

Policy analysts rarely enjoy the luxury of long and patient research. The immediacy of policy crisis does not permit it. Christopher Leman and Robert Nelson (1981), two economists experienced in federal policy analysis advise, "Dare to be quick and dirty . . . partial analysis, however dangerous, may be better than no analysis at all" (p. 103). The high opportunity costs of both policy analysts' and decision makers' time and the importance of many different decisions in which they are involved means employing the best methods in the time allotted and hoping for the best. The need for quick and dirty decisions more than anything separates policy analysts in academe from those working in government (Meltsner, 1976).

RULE 8: KNOW THE PLAYERS

Finding out who makes decisions is vital. Public decision making is "multi-layered and overlapping . . . with multiple access points" (Verdier, 1984, p. 425). There's rarely a single decision, but rather a complex process of consensus building between legislature, executive, and administrative agencies. Analysts must read newspapers and watch public affairs broadcasting and familiarize themselves with current issues and with entities and influential participants—legislative committees, commissions, departmental task forces, executive office staff. Often political advisors, outside government and hidden from the limelight, must also play a role. In fact, the news media may report vital policy information long before it reaches policy analysts' desks through regular channels. Policy analysts and even decision makers in the U.S. State Department read the *Washington Post* and *New York Times* religiously to find out issue positions, policy statements, and political decisions affecting them (Halperin, 1974).

Each participant plays a small and often ill-defined part. Legislators enact legislation without defining goals clearly—agreeing what to pass is difficult enough without specifying why (Verdier, 1984). *Log rolling—*

trading votes to secure favorable action on a project or policy—binds together all decisions, and many decision makers—appropriation, finance, and oversight committees—fight for jurisdiction (Amacher & Ulbrich, 1986). Governors or mayors take initiatives recondite of different things to different people. Analysts must be sensitive to these tensions.

On low-visibility, "closely held" issues, or those dominated by a few experienced decision makers, analytic results must be placed in the hands of the right players at the right time or their value may be lost forever. For highly visible and controversial issues, timing may be less critical. Analysts have more chance to provide information that shapes the debate (Weiss, 1992).

RULE 9: KNOW THE POLICY VOCABULARY

Civil Servant: "What I mean when I say that I am fully seized of
your aims and, of course will do my utmost to see that they're put
into practice. To that end, I recommend that we set up an
interdepartmental committee with fairly broad terms of reference
so that at the end of the day we'll be in a position to think through
the various implications and arrive at a decision based on
long-term considerations rather than rush prematurely into
precipitate and possibly ill-conceived action which
might well have unforeseen repercussions."
Departmental Secretary: "You mean no?"
Civil Servant: "Yes."
—Antony Jay and Jonathan Lynn, *Yes Minister* (BBC TV, 1981)

Public issues develop their own special vocabulary and any issue analysis must respect the current usage of words (Bonnett, 1994). What one state refers to as a "water transfer" another calls a "water trade"; what one program calls a "program completer" another terms a "graduate"; and a community college in one state is a technical school in another. These terms of art are not necessarily interchangeable. Experienced legislators or agency bureaucrats will be confused by analyses that misuse basic terms.

Terms are sensitive not only because they convey a specific technical meaning but because they have become the property of the participants in debates often laden with emotion. For example, *voucher* sometimes connotes the public subsidy of parochial schools. Ohio allows vouchers to be used for private schooling. Kentucky's governor changed the name of a new program he was introducing from "Job Training Vouchers"—which his staff recommended—to "Job Training Certificates." Enabling legislation passed. Public school choice advanced more rapidly in the late 1980s after debate was recast as one of "parental choice" rather than "education vouchers."

RULE 10: CONSIDER PLACEBOS

Although most policies are selected for their therapeutic impacts, analysts use *placebos* when there are no known cures or, more frequently, where the act of administering treatment, rather than treatment itself, helps the patient. A placebo may be necessary to make it politically feasible to pursue a strategy. In balancing the concerns of those displaced by development with the need to encourage innovation, for example, a placebo policy may be a vital ingredient. For example, programs to help firms adopt new technologies or to penetrate foreign markets could be used as placebos.

A placebo is not simply a way of doing nothing while appearing to meet political obligations. A placebo can also provide very real benefits. Medical research finds that placebos can alleviate headaches, rheumatism, motion sickness, and gastric hyperacidity. As much care should be devoted to the design of placebo policies as to genuinely therapeutic cures. Perhaps even more thought should be given to how they should be administered. Successful placebos should be cheap, should have minimal economic impacts (to reduce the risk of unintended consequences), and should be carried out with extensive publicity. For example, a museum of steelmaking constructed in Youngstown is a fitting tribute to the three generations of local steelmakers without the enormous cost of keeping steel plants open with public funds.

RULE 11: MEASURE OPTIONS IN TERMS
OF OPPORTUNITIES

The basic unit of analysis is the *opportunity*. Options are evaluated according to opportunities they create (their beneficial outcomes) and opportunities they destroy (their costs). Labor, bricks, and mortar used for a public works project or education services used in a public training program have alternative uses—opportunities that will be foregone if the project is built or the training program undertaken. These sacrifices constitute the cost or, more precisely, the *opportunity cost* of the policy under consideration. Evaluation must attempt to identify every major outcome, even though these do not all count as costs or benefits, because the political process must weigh each, especially redistributional consequences (who gains and who loses and how much).

Benefits are the value of opportunities created by the policy and must be compared against opportunities without the policy. Because of their diversity, benefits are generally harder to measure than costs. Ideally, we value them by summing how much each beneficiary would be willing to pay rather than do without them. Although we cannot measure this willingness directly—questionnaires are notoriously unreliable because nothing hinges on people correctly stating their preferences—market prices and patterns of behavior give us some clues. For example, user fees for services such as universities, parks, and libraries tell us the minimum amount that users were willing to pay for those services. Where the government provides a good that is also sold competitively—such as education—the market price (not the cost) is a good starting point for estimating the value of the benefits. If the government provides a good or service at no user cost, then we may be able to use the price of close substitutes that are privately marketed to "impute" a value, or *shadow price*. The net increase in property values in a subdivision served by a highway, for example, can be used to measure the value of the highway.

RULE 12. AVOID COMMON PITFALLS

The most common and often most serious errors in policy analysis arise not because outcomes are difficult to measure but because outcomes are inappropriately counted as costs and benefits. The Bureau of Reclamation was the first federal agency required to perform cost-benefit evaluations of all its large-scale projects. Although Congress hoped cost-benefit studies would deter unprofitable projects, it and related methodologies engendered several popular errors.

Error 1. To count construction jobs as public works project benefits

A public works project, whether a highway spur or a state office building, is often justified on the grounds that its construction will create jobs for the building trades and many more jobs when those workers spend their paychecks. But these jobs are not a measure of opportunities created. Jobs are an economic cost, not an economic benefit, of a project. They are an attractive political benefit—they inevitably enter the political consider-ation—especially since construction wages on public projects are often above the local average. Jobs should be treated as a *redistributive* outcome, not as a net economic benefit.

Jobs appear to be a net benefit because we overlook other jobs destroyed when raising money to pay for construction. Even if the federal government funds the project and the cost is spread among all federal taxpayers, jobs should not be the deciding factor. Funds still have an opportunity cost to the state or locality.

Even in a distressed community, where the project is explicitly under-taken to create jobs, many of those employed would have been working elsewhere had the project not been built. And those who would otherwise have been unemployed will not value their "opportunity" as equal to their paycheck—some pay is needed to compensate them for the burden of work. Overall, there is little in the construction workers' paychecks and even less in the lunch counter proprietor's earnings that can legitimately be counted as a benefit.

The object of economic development, that is, its benefits, ought to be the creation of *wealth*—measured as improved housing, public services, higher-paying productive jobs with benefits, cultural amenities, and so on (Thompson, 1972; Vaughan et al., 1984). Too often, policy analysts focus only on job creation, not wealth production. More jobs created in the short run may not be desirable. To take an extreme example, if policymakers wanted to end unemployment, they could outlaw the use of agricultural machinery forcing society to transfer labor to manual work in the fields. Building more efficient agricultural machinery and improving agricultural technology creates more wealth through better, more productive jobs (Laffer, 1996; Thompson, 1972).

Error 2. To select the project based on its costs and benefits to govern-ment

An evaluation of a tax abatement program to attract business will weigh costs (foregone taxes) against benefits (taxes paid by the business in coming years)(Weiwal, Persky, & Felsenstein, 1995). Although the exer-cise may be interesting, it does not establish the program's value. The government has no interest in the program separate from the interests of its citizens, and fiscal flow analysis ignores many of the project's costs and benefits those citizens may bear.

It may be useful to analyze the state's viewpoint about the costs and benefits of marketing programs to the legislature or the public. A program to reduce dependence among teenage children in low-income households by preventing pregnancy may be opposed because many of its "social" benefits appear nebulous. It might be more persuasive (once the executive is satisfied of the net social value of the program) to project savings from various social programs. A program should never be selected based on these considerations, however attractive. Full economic costs and benefits should be the basis of a policy analyst's evaluation.

Error 3. To assert that some outcomes—usually those that save or cost human lives—are too important to be measured in dollars

Although it is emotionally and even politically appealing to argue that no price is too high to save a human life, it does not reflect our true values or how we evaluate alternatives (Rhoads, 1985). If we really believed that a life has infinite value we would drive no faster than 10 miles an hour in a virtually indestructible automobile. Life-endangering and life-enhancing actions can be evaluated in the same way that we evaluate other actions. In Oregon, patients insured through Medicaid face rationing of health care that in effect places a specific upper dollar limit on their lives. Placing a dollar value on an outcome does not demean it. Dollars are simply the exchange rate among otherwise incomparable outcomes—a way of judging what opportunities we forego when we chose to follow a particular course of action.

Error 4. To overlook the fact that changes in property values capitalize many different project impacts

The increase in the value of property near a new road is the capitalized present value of the value of improved access, so it would be double counting to include as benefits both the increased property values and an estimate of the value of the saved travel time.

Many factors influence property values, from the quality of schools and the crime rate to the density of air pollution and the neighborhood noise level. This is to be expected: The decision to purchase a house normally involves the energetic collection of information by prospective buyers. Studies of systematic variations in housing prices have been used to estimate how people value different neighborhood amenities, such as clean air, quiet, low crime, and accessibility to downtown.

Error 5: To take into account past expenditures in evaluating opportunities

Policy analysts must resist taking into account past expenditures on projects when comparing policy alternatives (i.e., opportunity costs) taking effect in the future. Past expenditures are referred to as *sunk costs*. Consider an example: Policymakers fund a convention center year after year only to see it lose money. Policymakers reject funding for a new industrial park because they have already sunk so much money into the convention center and cannot turn back. The industrial park cannot compete with the convention center even though it might be the best expenditure for the future. All programs must be compared based on future returns on investment, not on past expenditures.

Although economically unjustifiable, sunk costs sometimes are taken into account solely for political reasons. Politicians cannot admit that past expenditures were wasted and that alternative future expenditures would be more desirable. Bureaucrats are also likely to resist this approach. In the 1970s, governments tried zero-based budgeting—a system requiring all agencies to justify expenditures from scratch. This approach attempted to correct the previous budgetary practice wherein agencies were awarded funding equivalent to the past year's allocation—referred to as the *base*, along with a portion of new moneys—called the *share*—for the upcoming year (Wildavsky & Caiden, 1997). A bird in the hand is worth two in the bush. This approach was dead before it could ever be tested in practice.

Error 6. To fail to build compensation for private property owners for takings by government

The government can take private property for the public good if it offers fair compensation to the property's owner. A recent trend in government is to deny private owners use of a portion of their property without compensation. Economists refer to this as a *taking*. For example, the private owner of a wetland by law must maintain the property for that purpose. In requiring that private land remain a wetland, its value is sometimes reduced to nothing. But the government, because it did not acquire the property outright through *eminent domain*, but only circumscribed its uses, is not required to offer compensation. This sidestepping of a constitutional right by the government will likely be a major policy issue in the coming years (Pollot, 1993).

Error 7. To fail to take into account adverse selection in implementing public programs

Adverse selection refers to the assumption of public services by people who need them but who were not originally targeted as clients: The result is greater, often unanticipated program expense (Stiglitz, 1988). For example: A public health agency sends a nurse door to door in a poor neighborhood to identify pregnant teenagers and refer them to prenatal care programs. In the process, the nurse finds elderly people in need of expensive, uncompensated medical attention that they would not have sought on their own. A program funded to help one client group unwittingly produces increased, possibly unreimbursed, costs for another. Analysts must anticipate adverse selection in calculating the costs and benefits of any program (see also, Lacker, 1994).

Error 8. To fail to take into account the costs and benefits of delegating policy or program authority

Governments, especially in an age of contracting out or funding nonprofits, use outside *agents* to act in their stead. In the British system, for example, the central government devolves authority to QANGOs (quasi-autonomous non-governmental organizations) to oversee everything from health care to arts programs ("Who's Really Who," 1998). Agents represent not only the governments, but also themselves. Agents can act contrary to the intentions of decision makers or their policies, creating in the process additional costs associated with among other things inefficiencies. A local government hires a firm to market the community only to learn that the firm is marketing itself and in effect wasting promotional resources. Policy analysis must anticipate these effects.

Error 9. To misunderstand the concept of market failure

Market failure refers to a situation in which a good or service is desired by society but is not provided or is distributed in insufficient quantities or at exorbitant prices because provision is not in the economic interest of private vendors or producers (Stiglitz, 1988). Policy analysts often use this argument to justify government intervention—the private sector cannot or will not act, therefore government must step in. In many cases, short of policy areas like the national defense, market failure can be a spurious argument for government intervention. Consider the construction of lighthouses. Because lighthouses help all ships and there is no way to collect fees for ships using them, they will not be constructed by the private sector (Coase, 1974). Yet, privately provided lighthouses were abundant in early America. In an age when government is *reinventing* itself through divestiture of public services to the private sector through contracting out, providing incentives, creating competition, and decentralizing ("Devolution Goes on Devolving," 1998; Osborne & Gaebler, 1992; Osborne & Plastrik, 1997), it may appear naive for policy analysts to argue market failure as a justification for public intervention.

Error 10. To initiate policy interventions contradicting policy goals

Without knowing it, usually out of carelessness, decision makers sometimes develop policy interventions that directly contradict policy goals. This results when decision makers fail to understand the nature of either the intervention or the goal. Consider state enterprise zones (Gravelle, 1992). Enterprise zones offer tax incentives to firms in distressed areas to create jobs for poor people (Ladd, 1994). Most zones offer subsidies to firms to lower the cost of plant and equipment. Yet, lowering the costs of production through capital incentives reduces employment: Firms substitute equipment for labor, eliminating rather than creating jobs.

Error 11. To assume that job creation is always the most important policy consideration

Decision makers promote policy by totting up jobs created, especially in economic development. But this may make no sense (Courant, 1994; Gravelle, Kiefer, & Zimmerman, 1992). The federal budget, as a consequence of the Budget Enforcement Act of 1990, is fixed once Congress passes a budget resolution. Expansion of an appropriation must be accompanied by an equivalent or greater reduction in other appropriations. Overall spending in the budget determines total employment in the economy. A new or expanded economic development program to create jobs therefore must be accompanied by a reduction in another program, causing an equivalent number of jobs to be lost. This being so, assessing programs based on job creation is not useful in helping decision makers choose one program over another. What would inform choice are factors like efficiency, distributional effects, or diversification, to name a few. So, a focus on jobs diverts attention away from the real crux of economic development—secondary goals only lightly touched on or ignored altogether.

RULE 13: COMPARE OPTIONS

Listing costs and benefits will be useful to some decision makers. Others, however, will call for "the bottom line." The best summary statistic for comparing programs that compete for public funds are the *net present value* and the *internal rate of return.*

Net Present Value

Net present value is the excess of discounted benefits over costs. When benefits and costs are properly discounted and adjusted for risk, the most attractive policy will have the largest net present value, in the absence of any other considerations. A disadvantage of the net present value criterion is that the results are sensitive to the discount rate used to discount benefits and costs. The higher the discount rate, the more attractive are policies producing immediate rather than long-term benefits. To allow for this, analysts usually estimate net present value with several plausible rates—such as 3%, 5%, and 10%—to determine how sensitive rankings are to the rate.

Sample of a Net Present Value Calculation

Year	Net Benefit	Discount Factor (with discount rate of 10%)	Present Value in Dollars
Present	100	1.00	100.00
After 1 year	70	.91	63.63
After 2 years	80	.83	66.08
After 3 years	100	.75	75.10

Internal Rate of Return

The internal rate of return treats program expenditures as an investment and measures the return. It is defined as that rate of discount that reduces the present value of the stream of net benefits to zero. Projects with the highest internal rate of return are most attractive. In many circumstances, both criteria yield the same ranking. Internal rate of return has the advantage of avoiding an assumption about the appropriate rate of discount. But it has many disadvantages—including the inability to chose among alternative projects on a fixed budget—and is less widely used than net present value (Gramlich, 1981).

Discounting the Future

Discounting future benefits and costs is important because people want compensation for sacrificing the benefits of goods and services today. Policy analysts can calculate discounts to estimate "present values." The rate should reflect the value in the best alternative use of funds required to pursue some policy. The federal government uses a 10% rate for most federal projects. Discounting is a rough estimate, but an approximate accounting of the time pattern of costs and benefits is preferable to none.

Discounting for Risk

Although we differ in our willingness to take risks, everyone requires compensation for taking risk. We prefer more to less certainty. Riskier assets, such as unrated bonds or venture capital investments, always compensate investors with a higher interest rate or rate of return. Policies that are "sure things" are more valuable than those promising similar benefits but with greater risk. Although risk assessment is difficult, an informal ranking by people familiar with the projects should enter into the final decision-making process.

Benefit-cost analysis is logical, but more an art than a science. The results depend on the reasonableness of assumptions, correct identification and classification of benefits and costs, and appropriate application of discounting criteria. The results can never be conclusive in favor of one policy. Decision makers, however, should be reluctant to support any policy that flunked a careful cost-benefit test.

RULE 14: FOCUS ON OUTCOMES, NOT PROCESS

Over the past decade, advocacy groups have become increasingly interested in *process*—the notion that good public policy can only be developed if all *stakeholders* are brought to the table, their concerns aired, and their needs accommodated. Not to take stakeholders into account could lead to the derailing of policy issues later in the policy process as those ignored take action or seek retribution. The first thing to note is that this concern is not new; what is new is the label stakeholders (Chenyoweth, 1995). Old-timers will recognize this as the common sense of politics. In the rush to take into account everybody's views in formal processes, policy analysts may spend so much time on the process that they ignore necessary work on the product—the policy. This goes hand in hand with a disturbing trend in some policy circles to treat process as an end in itself. For example, consultants to cities often use community leaders to help identify economic sectors that might, with public subsidies, produce jobs. When targets prove inappropriate, as they often do, consultants have been known to exclaim: "All is not lost, at least community leaders got to know one another and the local economy better." Or environmental groups may delay development by evoking rights to process. Process doesn't necessarily lead to a decision. This is dangerous for the policy analyst and decision maker, who often work under pressing deadlines not allowing for expanded process accommodation.

RULE 15: CONSIDER STARTING OVER

Some problems, such as inner-city decline, attract policy intervention after policy intervention across administrations until they make no sense or make matters worse. Economists refer to this as *government failure* in contrast to market failure (Ward & Deren, 1991). Some analysts believe, for example, that inner cities declined in part from a combination of public actions favoring suburbs: Interstate highways bypassed inner cities while allowing easy access to surrounding communities. Sewer, water, and other public utilities provided lifelines to suburbs to grow. Taxes in cities rapidly rose while public services deteriorated, making suburbs much more attractive. Home mortgage deductibility made home ownership in the suburbs a possibility for many Americans. In the wake of these policies, dependent, dysfunctional populations living in derelict neighborhoods grew. Urban renewal was an attempt to end dereliction by wholesale destruction of inner-city neighborhoods. Model cities followed, replacing vacant land with public housing, social services, low-income buildings, and universities. Enterprise zones, then empowerment zones, in turn followed, all to little or no avail.

Rather than piling one failed program on the next, policy analysts might consider starting over. Medicine offers an analog. Elderly patients see numerous specialists as they get older. Each specialist prescribes drugs for some conditions but not others. The specialists keep their own records, so no one knows what drugs patients are taking. Over time, prescriptions begin to interact, often in unpredictable and negative ways. Too often, this condition, *polypharmacy,* is treated with even more drugs. Geriatricians—physicians certified in treating elderly patients—frequently take patients off all drugs and begin to prescribe from scratch in a more reasonable way. The result: The patient's health improves.

RULE 16: KNOW WHEN TO GIVE UP

Policy analysts and decision makers sometimes continue to pursue policies that suit them, yet are detrimental to those the policies are intended to help. In medicine, the equivalent is summed up as, "The operation was a success, although the patient died." A contemporary parallel in policy is the debate on health insurance. No credible person believes that the health care system is working as it should. It's expensive, inequitable, and wasteful. It must be mended. But a consistent drumbeat to socialize the system never ceases, even when it's clear that most people do not like this option. Too many people believe that Medicaid, Medicare, veteran's hospitals, and public health clinics—all versions of social medicine—are not part of the solution but represent a large part of the problem. President Clinton realized that a wholesale reworking of health care as proposed by Hillary Clinton would not sell but was able to achieve many of his goals through piecemeal reforms and devolution. Clinton's proposals to allow people 55 to 61 years of age to purchase health insurance under Medicare, to establish a patient's bill of rights, and to fund increased child health care represent his incremental approach (see Chait, 1998; Goodman & Matthews, 1998).

RULE 17: DEVELOP A COMMUNICATIONS STRATEGY FOR THE POLICY

"Without publicity, there can be no public support. And without public support," warned British Prime Minister Benjamin Disraeli, "every nation must decay." Unfortunately, publicity is rarely a skill at which policy analysts excel. With strong conceptual skills, policy analysts judge issues on their merits. They may even be irritated when the media or the public insist on reducing good ideas to their absurd extremes. In 1972, the presidential candidate George McGovern advocated a negative income tax, a perfectly respectable policy for eliminating the 100% (or higher) marginal tax rate that welfare recipients then faced if they accepted work. The policy had earlier been supported by Milton Friedman, a leading conservative economist and later Nobel laureate. But the proposal did not emerge as a conservative idea. Senator McGovern wanted to give everyone, regardless of income, a check for several thousand dollars, a *spin* on the negative income tax its proponents never intended. While the candidate tried to get the story straight, the campaign lost valuable momentum.

But, in 1980, the presidential candidate George Bush failed to discredit rival candidate Ronald Reagan's economic proposals to cut taxes and increase defense spending by characterizing the plan as "voodoo economics." Reagan had already communicated a plausible explanation for his policies with the public. Tax cuts stimulate economic growth, which if high enough produces more revenues even at lower tax rates. Ironically, years later, Bush was forced, albeit unsuccessfully in his defeat by the candidate Bill Clinton, to defend "voodoo economics."

Communication, therefore, is vital for two reasons: first, to get your story in the public's mind before it gets hold of the wrong version; and second, to persuade the public that your policies are understood as plausible solutions to the problem (Majchrzak, 1984).

To treat problems effectively—whether inflamed appendixes or increased unemployment—healers need to find causes and to predict consequences of alternative remedies. Because guesswork rarely enjoys a run of luck long enough to attract repeat customers and exhaustive scientific tests are often infeasible or too costly, healers need to simplify complex systems they wish to treat into a model convenient for diagnosis and treatment.

The model must be communicated to the patient. Patients, however, cannot easily judge the efficacy of a doctor's techniques any more than voters can judge the effectiveness of the economic model employed by an elected leader. They rely on physicians whose technique "express[es] so-called scientific principles which are widely accepted if not intelligently appreciated" (Miller, 1978, p. 56). If patients do not accept the rationale on which the physician's authority rests, they turn away.

The policy analyst faces a similar challenge. A political leader will neither win legislative support nor receive public credit for policies unless he or she succeeds in communicating the implicit model on which the strategy is based. The drifting away of a physician's patients has an obvious analogy in losing legislative votes and, ultimately, public support. Policy statements need not and cannot be economics seminars. But they should contain relevant aspects of the model in statements about causes and reasons for proposing a solution. This can inspire public confidence that the proposed remedy has a fighting chance.

There are many examples of leaders winning election and reelection based on their own charismatic power to persuade people of their capacity as a "healer" without divulging the scientific framework undergirding their powers. This is, however, a rare feat, sometimes beyond the leaders wrestling with economic issues today.

SUMMARY

Once policy analysts or physicians determine the likely cause of a problem presented to them, inevitably they must select from what can be a wide variety of treatments. For physicians, treatments include doing nothing, surgery, radiation, or medication. In each treatment mode, numerous opportunities abound, with benefits and liabilities to patients—and caregivers, for that matter. Policy analysts, also in the face of a range of options, must lay out pros and cons of each so that the decision makers may wisely choose. In evaluating treatment possibilities, policy analysts must look at priorities, risks, costs, and benefits at present and in the future. For each option, policy analysts must know its vocabulary, supporters and detractors, and timetable for proposal and implementation. Policy analysts must consider offering citizens placebos when other actions are undesirable; they must know when to start over in pursuing policy solutions and when to give up. Once they've laid out the options for the decision makers, they must decide how the problem and policy solution can be communicated to build support or minimize likelihood of failure.

CASE STUDIES

To compare programs and policies, we must create *scenarios* (see, especially, Cook, Osterholt, & Riley, 1988). This means using information about existing programs to project what is likely to happen as a result of the proposed action. Although impact categories can usually be identified, predicting their magnitude must often be a matter of conjecture.

Policy analysis is a systematic way of developing these scenarios. But the technique is sometimes misused—out of error and/or out of excessive zeal for the project. Consider two examples: one, an initiative to deal with unemployment among minority youth; the other, the construction of a new highway link.

Case Study 1. Youth Unemployment

Persistent poverty in some communities, particularly among young minorities, has spawned numerous jobs programs. There are over two decades of experience with such initiatives; new ones can build on this history. The first step in this retrospective evaluation is to list all possible program consequences. The economist Steven Rhoads (1985) provides a concise description of important outcomes:

> The benefits of job training programs accrue both to those enrolled and to the rest of society. Those enrolled gain through higher post-training earnings, and, perhaps, through intangible self-image gains from reduced dependence on government charity, on drugs or alcohol, and on unlawful income. The rest of society gains through use of goods and services

produced during training, through increased taxes generated by trainees'
post-program income, through lower costs of welfare, drug, and alcoholism programs, and through the intangible psychic gains of helping the
disadvantaged make their way in the world. (p. 129)

The difficult part is to place probable values on these outcomes (either
retrospectively or prospectively). What percentage of program participants
would not have found jobs in the program's absence? What would the likely
incidence of alcoholism be in the absence of the program? Data needed to
answer these questions may be provided by surveys, statistical procedures,
or even guesswork. By comparing hypothetical outcomes with actual
participant experiences, program effects can, in principle, be deduced. In
practice, it may be difficult to reach a consensus on "what would have
been." An alternative, in such instances as the jobs program discussed by
Rhoads (1985), may be to identify a "control" group having similar traits
to those of the trainees and use them for comparison.

Policy outcomes depend on the health of the national and state economies, but the magnitudes of these influences are difficult to assess. To
accommodate this uncertainty, the analyst creates alternative scenarios for
different economic assumptions.

Many policy effects are indirect and are not measurable in cash flows.
For example, streamlining state permitting procedures saves businesses
money, but there is no item on their balance sheet attributable to the policy.
Nevertheless, these impacts should be listed. A rough allocation of a youth
jobs program's outcomes between costs and benefits might look like this:

	Individual	Others	Society
BENEFITS			
Gain in earnings after tax	x	x	
Future increase in taxes paid		x	x
Nonmonetary satisfaction	x		x
COSTS			
Tuition costs	x		x
Scholarship costs		x	x
Higher living expenses	x		x
Earnings foregone after taxes	x		x
Taxes foregone		x	x
Transfer payments foregone	x	x	

If people are paid commensurate to the value of their work, increases in earnings measure gains in participants' productivity. Part of this gain is enjoyed by the participants and part by society through higher taxes. Program costs include explicit costs such as tuition and scholarships, but also hidden sacrifices such as higher living costs from participants living away from home, for example.

Reductions in transfer payments as participants find work show up as a benefit to society (the saved tax revenues) but a corresponding, and exactly offsetting, cost to those who no longer receive them. That is why transfer payments "net out" from cost-benefit analyses. Creating opportunity for the poor is a valuable program outcome, but there is no way to assign a dollar value to the transfer of money among recipients. The value of redistribution is weighed in the political process.

Case Study 2. Building a Highway Link

The level and quality of infrastructure investments and the effectiveness of maintenance programs influence regional economic growth potential and its ability to respond to changing environments. The Urban Institute, a policy think tank in Washington, D.C., typically analyzes 11 factors when evaluating projects under grants and contracts, although not all belong in cost-benefit calculations.

We cannot calculate benefits and costs simply by adding all items that appear favorable and subtracting those that do not. If all the impacts listed below were assigned to either the cost or benefit columns, there would be dramatic double and even triple counting. Those items preceded by (+) should properly be considered benefits, those with (−), costs, and those with (0) are real impacts but should not be added in cost-benefit analyses— either because they are redistributive or because they have been taken into account in one of the other variables. (In this example, the environmental costs under Category 4 are assumed to be reflected in changes in property values at the affected locations.) Analysts should quantify as many effects as possible, including those that do not belong in a cost-benefit study, because balancing them is the heart of political decision-making. Following are the 11 factors the Urban Institute uses:

1. Fiscal Impacts (on expenditures and revenues)

(−) The state will incur planning, land acquisition, and construction costs.

(−) The state will also incur a stream of maintenance and repair expenditures into the future.

(0) The state may experience increased gasoline sales taxes and other travel related revenues (this would be a + if the revenues come from out-of-state drivers).

(0) Local governments will gain increased property taxes from the increase in property values adjacent to the highway; those further from the road may experience a decline.

(0) Local governments will lose property tax payments on the land absorbed by the highway.

2. Health and Safety Effects

(+) Motorists will have a safer, more comfortable, and faster ride.

3. Community Economic Effects

(0) Communities along the highway will experience increases in economic activity and residential population; those not on the highway may shrink.

(−) Some access roads may become more congested.

(+) Other roads will become less congested.

(0) The economic value (i.e., as farmland, residential land, or manufacturing space) of the land absorbed will be lost.

(+) The value of some land near the highway will increase because of improved accessibility.

(−) The value of some land near the highway will decrease because of environmental deterioration.

(0) Local construction workers will be employed.

(0) There will be a temporary boom in sales of food and other items during the construction phase.

4. Environmental, Aesthetic, and Social Effects

(0) Air quality along the highway's corridor will deteriorate; the quality in those areas relieved of congestion may improve.

(0) Noise levels near the highway will increase (and may decline elsewhere).

(0) The views of overlooking residential and commercial property may be impaired.

5. Disruption and Inconvenience Caused by Project

(−) During construction, local traffic will be subject to delays.

(−) Noise and dirt will be greatly increased during construction.

6. Distributional Effects—Who Is Affected and How Much

(0) The primary beneficiaries are those traveling frequently between locations along the highway and those who own land that increases in value as a result of the project.

(0) Those bearing a disproportionate burden will include taxpayers not using the road and those whose property falls in value (e.g., because of a loss of view or noise).

(0) Construction workers will gain if they are paid a wage that is considerably above what they earn elsewhere.

7. Feasibility, Including Public Support and Project Readiness

n.a. List of local groups still opposed/in favor of the highway.

8. Implications of Deferring Project

n.a. Saved development and construction expenditure.

n.a. An additional year of congestion on other roads, more accidents, and environmental harm.

9. Amount of Uncertainty and Risk

(−) Some projected use of the road depends on uncertain factors such as a local plant staying open, or the completion of a major residential development. Uncertainty is a cost.

(−) Are there geological problems that might inflate costs?

(−) Might the proposed highway be obsolete after a few years if growth accelerates slightly?

(−) Is there a chance that the highway will generate enough new auto trips to endanger the ability of the area to comply with clean air standards?

10. Effects on Interjurisdictional Relations

(0) The jurisdictions that are net losers from highway will expect compensation in the future (in the form of a state park, an industrial park, etc.).

11. Advantages Accruing From Relationship With Other Capital Projects

(+) Improves access to state park, which is being expanded.

(+) Will allow channelization of stream that currently floods every 5 years.

5

Prognosticating

Nomination for the best forecast of the 20th Century: John Maynard Keynes, in The Economic Consequences of the Peace *(1919), warns that the Allied Powers' harsh treatment of Germany after World War I will lead the country to bankruptcy so devastating that it will launch another World War even more destructive than the first.*

Decision makers prospectively shape policy by anticipating economic and social scenarios and consequences of alternative actions. Physicians refer to this stage in patient management as prognostication, asking what are likely outcomes of the treatment strategy for the patient. Successful forecasting—the policy analyst's label for prognosticating—requires combining the analytic power of statistical models with the advantages of intuitive judgments to make assumptions about the future explicit. Even though the Federal Reserve Bank employs the most sophisticated econometric models in forecasting economic trends, federal monetary policy remains grounded in the intuitive judgments of the current chairman, Alan Greenspan (Wessel, 1997). Physicians do much the same with medical decision-making protocols, many of which reside in computers and employ statistical probability. Disagreement over how to address a problem may be based not on differences over the consequences of actions so much as on differences over the assumptions about economic events. When assumptions are explicit, consistent public policies can be better developed. Governments, like businesses, must operate with much uncertainty, but good forecasting helps manage that uncertainty.

Forecasting techniques range from discussions among policy analysts over the probabilities of alternative scenarios to surveys of agency staff over projected caseloads and computerized output from complex simulation models. Physicians often consult with peers or specialists, especially when there is uncertainty or liability. Techniques have different strengths and weaknesses and vary according to the analytic skills—computing,

75

statistical, modeling—they require from users, time required to derive results, and cost (Georgoff & Murdick, 1986). Policy analysts employ a variety of forecasting techniques to see which performs best or to locate points of convergence or divergence. This chapter offers rules about how to use forecasts in policy analysis targeted to decision makers. It briefly reviews different forecasting enterprises, laying out techniques and discussing methodological strengths and weaknesses—others have undertaken much more intense work in this field.

Why Forecast?

Policy analysts need forecasts to (a) predict annual revenue streams; (b) estimate fiscal, economic, political, and social impacts of policy interventions; (c) respond to forecasts made by others, especially opponents or advocates; and (d) support strategic, long-range, and tactical planning.

1. Predicting the Economic Environment

Most government agencies forecast their overall economic conditions for 2 to 5 years. These are used to make revenue forecasts (below) and as the basis for program forecasts by individual agencies. State forecasts can easily be computed from national forecasts, perhaps by assuming that the output and the employment of the state's main industries remains a constant fraction of those at the national level. More sophisticated regional models are available for many areas. State forecasters can refine this approach to accommodate shifts in the state's relative strength with respect to each industry in as great a detail as resources and patience allow. Forecasts of employment by industry and occupation are used for program planning, administration, and evaluation; career counseling and guidance; job creation and placement; marketing; client representation at disability hearings; and database development (Lawrence & Bergman, 1985).

2. Forecasting Revenues

Revenues must be forecast annually and require modeling of complex relationships between changes in economic variables—state income, employment, mineral production, and retail sales, for example, and revenues yielded by different taxes. Therefore, most states use econometric or input-output models to make revenue forecasts. In some states, the legislature, the budget office, and other executive offices all make forecasts. The models are very different from longer-run economic models because they have a short time horizon, 6 to 8 quarters, and must forecast tax bases that are not usually included in economic models. States relying on mineral royalties or dominated by a single industry need to perform specific, in-depth analyses of those sectors of their economies.

3. Forecasting for Policy Analysis

Formal models can be useful for studying possible effects of proposed changes in state taxes or in other policies, especially where these effects involve complex interactions among industries or regions. Frequently, the decision to propose a major policy change hinges on an assessment of the health of a particular sector or area or on the expected rate of employment growth or income in the state. Will economic growth be strong enough to reduce poverty and unemployment below target levels? How many communities will be hit by plant closings resulting from foreign competition? How will cutbacks in federal funds affect income in different communities? These forecasts must usually be augmented by an analyst's judgment.

4. Forecasting for Planning

Although most forecasting concerns predicting the values of today's variables in the future, one branch anticipates issues that will become important. Some issues begin as headlines—the failure of a savings and loan, the collapse of a bridge, or a damaging storm; others emerge slowly—our awareness of the danger of environmental pollutants, for example. Scientific research raises the possibility of harm—from exposure to lead in automobile emissions and use of the insecticide DDT—but awareness grows slowly, sometimes accelerated by chronic episodes, until it finally becomes a public policy issue.

Strategic forecasts embody the administration's considered judgments about the future. Therefore, senior staff must choose among different scenarios. Where there are strongly divergent views—over the future of a traditional industry, for example—the governor may convene task forces or commissions to frame alternative views of the future and identify strategic problems.

Analysts may want to use forecasts to anticipate problems before they have matured into crises. Many problems, however, cannot be addressed until they have become crises. It did not require sophisticated forecasts to predict that underinvestment in public infrastructure would lead, eventually, to a deteriorating quality of life and a growing number of accidents. Yet, arousing the public and mobilizing agencies and legislatures before the worst happened has proved very difficult. It is not enough to anticipate problems. Forecasts must be accompanied by strategies to build public support for action.

Who Should Forecast?

Embodying forecasts in the policy-making process raises administrative issues—in federal, state, or local government as in other large nonprofit or quasi-governmental organizations. First, there are many different users of forecasts, each with different time horizons, forecast variables, and deadlines. A state labor department, for example, makes 10-year forecasts under a federal statistics program that are used by the education department to support vocational education budget requests and school construction decisions. Human services agencies make county and local projections of at-risk populations, mostly annually. Local school districts make projections of future school enrollments, often using estimates prepared by consultants. The corrections department forecasts prison populations, the planning office forecasts economic and demographic variables, and the budget office predicts revenues. These forecasts may be widely divergent, yet millions of dollars of expenditure depend on them.

Many states obtain state and national forecasts from national consulting firms that offer modeling, data access, and data management services. Most users have found the forecasts relatively poor but they maintain contracts for access to the enormous databases these firms offer. Some states claim that finding the flaws in these "scaled down" national models proved valuable. The model may be a useful "starting kit" for the state. Unfortunately, there are few comparative analyses of the performance of the leading proprietary models at the state level. It is unlikely that any state's forecasting needs can be met wholly through a proprietary model, however large or expensive.

A state forecasting team must develop confidence in the forecast process, not in individual forecasts or forecasters. Because different agencies are interested in widely different outcomes of the model, they will use it only if they understand broadly how the model works and trust its operators to produce objective analyses.

Most states locate their forecasting program in a staff rather than a line agency to avoid the temptation to manipulate forecast models in the interests of the agency's own programs. Regular consultation with a panel of experts can bring fresh insights and encourage the staff to produce high-quality work. The forecast should be seen as the possession of the state rather than as an instrument through which a particular group gains power.

There are limits to what can be publicly forecast, because of the sensitivity of some issues. For example, a widely publicized forecast that the local banking system was threatened—perhaps as a result of difficulties in an important local industry such as oil or agriculture—may precipitate a run on the banks requiring state intervention. But the process must allow bad news to surface. Most public officials believe that they must be optimistic because their buoyant attitude will be reflected in real economic gains. Yet, if bad news surfaces in the administration's office, the administration will have more control over the issue than if it waits for the patient to show up in the waiting room. But tact is vital when transmitting a downbeat forecast to an employer. And it requires some statesmanship to acknowledge problems publicly.

Policy analysts must often respond to forecasts made by other units of government and interest groups that may have concerns quite different from those motivating state policy. For example, federal predictions of the demand for coal will affect economic activity, revenues, and local government planning in coal-producing states and will change the underlying assumptions about the costs and benefits of strip mine reclamation and about power plant emissions controls. On the other hand, predictions made by the U.S. Department of Agriculture about future lumber shortages may stimulate interest in state programs to promote tree planting.

Local utilities issue forecasts about future demands for electricity as part of campaigns to win a rate increase. Business groups produce models that show that unless taxes are reduced and other measures taken to improve the state's business climate, investment will fall and unemployment rise. A single manufacturer may hire a prestigious economic consulting firm to show that because of weak demand and fierce competition it cannot comply with the state's sulfur emission standards without jeopardizing jobs.

What Forecasting Techniques Are Available and Work Best?

Policy analysts can forecast in many different ways. The professors David M. Georgoff and Robert G. Murdick list 20 different techniques that business managers could employ and analyzed the strengths and weaknesses of each (Georgoff & Murdick, 1986; see also Sylvia, Sylvia, & Gunn, 1997). Their results are summarized below, adapted to reflect the perspective of policy analysts. Georgoff and Murdick classify forecasting techniques under four types: *judgment, counting, time-series,* and *association* or *causal* methods. The description of each of these 20 techniques invariably involves some technical language, but to avoid that would involve extremely lengthy descriptions.

Judgment

Naive extrapolation: The application of a simple assumption about the economic outcome in the next time period, or a simple, if subjective, extension of the results of current events.

Sampling: A compilation of estimates by administrators or local governments of expected case loads, capacity needs, and so on, adjusted for presumed biases and expected changes in relevant variables.

Jury of executive opinion: The consensus of a group of "experts," often from a variety of functional areas in the state.

Scenario methods: Smoothly unfolding narratives that describe an assumed future expressed through a sequence of time-series snapshots.

Delphi technique: A successive series of estimates independently developed by a group of "experts," each member of which, at each step, uses a summary of the group's previous results to formulate new estimates.

Historical analogy: Predictions based on elements of past events that are analogous to the present situation.

Counting Methods

Market testing: Responses of representative users of new policies or public facilities, tested and extrapolated to estimate the policy's prospects.

Consumer market survey: Attitudes and use intentions gathered from representative users of a program or public facility.

Industrial market survey: Similar to the previous method but using expert subjects, resulting in more informed (but potentially less objective) evaluations.

Time-Series Methods

Moving averages: Recent values of forecast variables averaged to predict future outcomes.

Exponential smoothing: An estimate for the coming period based on a constantly weighted combination of the forecast estimate for the previous period and the most recent outcome.

Adaptive filtering: A derivation of a weighted combination of actual and estimated outcomes, systematically altered to reflect data pattern changes.

Time-series extrapolation: A prediction of outcomes derived from projecting past data into the future—usually using the future extension of a least squares function fitted to a data series that uses time as an independent variable.

Time-series decomposition: A prediction of expected outcomes from trend, seasonal, cyclical, and random components, which are isolated from a data series.

Box-Jenkins: A complex, computer-based iterative procedure that produces an auto-regressive, integrated, moving average model, adjusts for seasonal and trend factors, estimates appropriate weighting parameters, tests the model, and repeats the cycle as appropriate.

Association or Causal Methods

Correlations: Predictions of values based on historic patterns of covariation between variables.

Regression models: Estimates produced from a predictive equation derived by minimizing the residual variance of one or more predictor (independent) variables.

Leading indicators: Forecasts generated from one or more preceding variables that are systematically related to the variable to be predicted.

Econometric models: Outcomes forecast from an integrated system of simultaneous equations that represent relationships among elements of the national economy derived from combining history and economic theory.

Input-output models: A matrix model that indicates how demand changes in one industry can directly and cumulatively affect other industries.

The strengths and weaknesses of each technique are indicated below. The route to good forecasting is to match what is needed from the forecast with the technique offering those characteristics most effectively.

Judgment

Econometric models—a set of mathematical relationships among data related to the state economy—may present the greatest difficulty to those without technical training. They include the time-series and association or causal methods described above. Econometric models can be as simple as a single equation in which sales tax revenues over the next 18 months are determined by national predictions of GDP or as complex as the large national models with hundreds of equations. They can project complex scenarios quickly and objectively but cannot evaluate how reasonable these scenarios are and cannot check on the quality of the current data used to project the future.

Since all models are conditional statements about relationships, the way that the relationship is structured determines how well it works. For example, to determine the future viability of the unemployment insurance fund, a model may be constructed in which state employment is a function of national employment growth over the next 5 years—forecasts of the latter variable are readily available either from private modeling firms or from the U.S. Department of Commerce. But what is the nature of the relationship? If the national rate of employment growth doubles, does the state rate also double? Is the relationship symmetrical? That is, does a 1% decline in the national growth rate reduce state employment growth as much as a 1% increase raises it? The usual way of answering these questions is to look at how the two variables behaved in the past—but this implicitly assumes that the relationship will continue unchanged.

The advent of the personal computer has placed modeling within reach of all states. In fact, by aiming at models that fit on a personal computer, states can avoid the most expensive forecasting mistake, which is to believe that the larger a model, and the more closely its equations seem to reflect the real economy, the more accurate will be the forecast.

Not only are cheaper and smaller models just as accurate as larger models, they are also much easier to use. If a systematic approach to forecasting is to permeate many parts of policy analysis, then a model that can be easily duplicated on a floppy disk will be very useful.

Building from a core model allows some of the idiosyncrasies of the state to be included. For example, most regional models predicted that, in the short run, the result of quotas on the importation of Japanese automobiles would be an increase in output and employment of the transportation equipment sector, SIC 37. But in Maine, where almost all of SIC 37 is shipbuilding, this relationship would be ignored.

The developers of the state econometric model in Maine offer the following guidelines for anyone starting out building a policy forecasting model (Irland, Cogan, & Lawton, 1984):

1. Don't contract out for more than model operation and computations. In-house users should be involved in setting some of the parameters to suit the state's needs.
2. Set priorities. There will always be a long list of interesting projects. Identify those that are crucial to improve the model's overall accuracy before pursuing less central submodels.
3. Write reports for interested nontechnical readers to draw many people into the forecasting process.
4. Avoid using the model to recommend specific policies—but spell out the implications of alternatives.
5. Present bad news carefully and constructively, but don't try to hide it.

6. Involve a team of private sector people who can provide a different perspective and ask tough questions.

Errors can enter a forecasting model in many ways. First, exogenous forecasts (national employment, in the example above) may not be good. Second, the relationship between exogenous variables and state variables may be misspecified (it may have changed recently, so that estimates based on past behavior are no longer valid). Third, important variables may have been omitted and thus not captured in the model. Trial, error, and, most of all, experience will help you adapt forecasts as the economic environment changes.

Forecasting models are, by their nature, limited to "measurable" factors. But some of the most important aspects of the economy are not directly observable. The most common way of entering the unmeasurable into the model is to gather a panel of people involved in forecasting and use their judgment to modify the exogenous forecasts or suggest reasons for trying different specifications for relationships (Cook et al., 1988). For example, the panel might suggest that a change in the state's industrial structure has altered its link to the national economy or that a rapid increase in the labor force participation has brought the state up to the national average and therefore the state's labor force will grow more slowly relative to the nation in the future. These suggestions will be reflected in the various scenarios fed to the model.

Judgment should be used cautiously. Georgoff and Murdick (1986; see also Sjoberg, 1982) conclude:

> While many quantitative forecasts incorporate some subjectivity, fore-casters should rely more heavily on the output of a quantitative forecast than on their own judgment. Forecasting research has concluded that even simple quantitative techniques outperform the unstructured intuitive assessments of experts and that using judgment to adjust the values of a quantitatively derived forecast will reduce its accuracy. This is so because intuitive predictions are susceptible to bias and managers are limited in their ability to process information and maintain consistent relationships among variables. (p. 115)

The forecaster should incorporate subjective judgments in dynamic situations when the quantitative models do not reflect significant internal and external changes. Even in these cases, the forecaster should incorporate subjective adjustments as inputs in the model rather than adjusting the model's final outcome.

When confronted with extended horizons or with novel situations involving limited data and no historical precedent, judgment or accounting methods should be used. Applying judgment in such situations, however, should be done on a structured basis—quantitative techniques should be used to test and support assumptions.

Some companies marketing econometric models have oversold their capabilities. During recent years, many forecasting services adjusted their 1995 economic forecasts in response to short-run changes in economic conditions—downward during the 1982 recession and upward again when the 1984 boom emerged. This reveals either a misunderstanding of the nature of long-run modeling or a misspecified model.

How Accurate Are Forecasts?

The Bureau of Labor Statistics recently funded a study to evaluate the accuracy of state projections made between 1977 and 1979 of employment by industry and occupation in 1982 (Cruze et al., 1985). The findings provide a useful guide for states:

1. All states used either linear regression or shift-share models to develop their projections, but all adjusted their models' projections with analysts' judgments.

2. The mean projection error for all 3-digit SIC industries was 22.6% (generally, the higher the level of disaggregation, the larger the projection error). The direction of the employment shift was correctly predicted two thirds of the time.

3. The errors were greatest in those industries that had experienced the largest increases or decreases in employment up to 1982.

4. Regression models yielded higher errors than shift-share analysis.

5. Substate projections were less accurate than statewide ones, and national projections by BLS were more accurate than state ones.

6. Linear regression models specified differently for each industrial sector overall did not yield more accurate 1982 projections than the standard regression model of state industry employment regressed against national employment and time. Customized models were a little better than standard models for industries in which employment changed moderately and did perform better for substate areas.

7. Projections for occupations were of similar accuracy to industry projections. They were better for occupations in which employment changed moderately. Manufacturing occupations were projected more accurately than nonmanufacturing ones.

These evaluations are a vital source of information for preparing to develop a forecasting model. No amount of economic expertise or computer hardware can guarantee forecasts. The economist Robert Clower (1995) lamented, "If serious prediction were the sole criterion of a science, economics would long ago have ceased to exist as a serious intellectual pursuit" (p. 51). But some of the popular disillusionment with economists as forecasters is a result of expecting too much. We do not ask physicians to predict when we will die—merely to forecast what actions on our part are likely to prolong or shorten our lives. It is almost impossible for any economic model to predict the values of certain economic variables into the future—there are too many factors that can change. It is more reasonable to treat forecasts as conditional predictions—that is, what will happen to a few variables under different policies, all other things being equal? With these forecasting features in mind, we offer five rules to guide policy analysts.

RULE 1: GARBAGE IN YIELDS GARBAGE OUT

Good forecasting data are difficult to obtain. Forecasts often require numbers that extend over long periods of time, represent short time intervals (i.e., days, weeks, or months are preferred, but annual are often the norm), are compatible with other forecasts or data, are timely or readily available, and are valid and reliable, not to mention satisfying technical requirements and assumptions.

Although forecasting results attract the most attention—especially for decision makers lacking understanding of forecasting technicalities—it is really the quality of the data that matters. A forecast is only as good as the data it is based on (Pedhazur & Schmelkin, 1991). Policy analysts conducting or using forecasts must satisfy themselves that the data are of sufficient quality to warrant use in policy analysis.

RULE 2: USE MULTIPLE TECHNIQUES TO FORECAST, THEN LOOK FOR CONVERGENCE

Forecasting techniques—reviewed in previous sections—have strengths and weaknesses. No forecast is superior to all others. This is one reason why the policy arena produces so many different forecasts from different sources. Everyone thinks he or she can forecast better. Policy analysts are likely to have competing forecasts in need of reconciliation.

Policy analysts should look for convergence in forecasting results. When different forecasts converge, analysts may be more confident in their accuracy. When analysts control forecasting resources, they should purposefully forecast with different methodologies, looking for convergence.

Consumers of forecasting information should be cautious. Consensus forecasts of basic economic data from national brokerage firms can result from intentional bias rather than legitimate forecasts (Bleakley, 1997). A study by the Federal Reserve Bank of New York (Bleakley, 1997) showed that national banks offering forecasts were accurate. Security firms and independent forecasters were inaccurate. The reason: Security firms and independents want rosier forecasts to encourage investors to buy stocks and bonds. Banks do not sell these products.

RULE 3: WHEN FORECASTS DIVERGE, CONSIDER AVERAGING THEM

In the real world of noise and error, forecasts are likely to diverge, diluting any confidence policy analysts might have in them. But even divergent forecasts can be salvaged. In Ohio, for example, the Office of Budget and Management (OBM) contracted with an outside vendor to forecast state revenues. OBM also invited analysts from across the state to bring their forecasts to Columbus and evaluate the vendor's work. OBM took the vendor forecast and 10 other forecasts, averaging them to yield the Ohio's official revenue estimate. Statisticians will recognize that the average, ceteris paribus, is the point of least error. In Ohio, averaged forecasts turned out to be highly accurate.

Sometimes, having too many forecasts can be a nightmare for policy analysts and decision makers. Consider another Ohio example. State and federal funding is often allocated to communities based on population size and poverty level. The larger the poverty population, the greater the need for outside funding. Knowing this, local organizations, representing governments, advocacy groups, nonprofits, associations, and the like all produce forecasts to maximize funding transferred from higher levels of government. Because forecasting is not scientific and because it is difficult to police or control, the state government was bombarded with population forecasts, all of which could not be accurate. Additionally, some local areas were left out, not having the capacity to produce or purchase their own competing forecast. Having no way to sort out the wheat from the chaff, the decision makers created a special data center that issues official population numbers for all local areas in the state. Organizations requesting outside funds were obligated to use official numbers, even though they may have had better forecasts from other sources.

RULE 4: LOOK FOR TURNING POINTS

Even experienced forecasters make two common mistakes.

Error 1. Assume that trends in the past will hold in the future

The past is often a reliable predictor of the future, but not always. Forecasts that merely extrapolate the past into the future are especially dangerous ("America Extrapolated," 1992). Consider an example from Ohio State University (OSU). In the late 1960s, OSU administrators observed that throughout the decade enrollments were rapidly escalating, straining university campus housing capacity. Researchers took the annual growth in enrollment, extrapolated it into the 1970s and 1980s, and concluded that 10,000 new dorm spaces were needed. These spaces, and more, were constructed. At what were to be peak years of demand for dorms, enrollments precipitously declined, forcing OSU to convert new dorm space into university offices. Skeptics claim that this was planned by administrators to secure better office space. But what really happened was that the researchers did not take into account the fact that baby boomers— who created the demand for dorm space—were to be followed by baby busters, a much smaller cohort of young people than the boomers. Had the researchers broken enrollments down by age cohort and then looked at trends, they would have seen the turning point. Always look for turning points.

Error 2. Assume that the world is linear

A second common mistake, related to the example above ("America Extrapolated," 1992), is to assume that the world is linear—that is, that general trends always move in straight lines, even though any given data point may fluctuate above or below the general trend. Although linearity makes life easier not only on forecasters but also for policy analysts and decision makers, the world relevant to policy is generally nonlinear.

One reason analysts persist in assuming linearity is that many of the statistical software packages on which they were trained are linear models. Another reason is that the complexity of the mathematics involved in nonlinear modeling extends beyond the skills of many analysts. And nonlinear models are difficult to explain to laypersons, or even social scientists generally. Policy analysts must find the capacity to go beyond linear modeling when necessary or risk being wrong. Again, look for turning points!

RULE 5: MONITOR FORECASTS USING PROSPECTIVE DATA

The goal of forecasting is accuracy. One way to achieve this is to continually evaluate forecast results as actual data become available. With real data, models can be evaluated and revised as necessary, and continual monitoring allows decision makers to change course should forecast results appear inaccurate.

Continual monitoring may be difficult. Forecasting models are complicated, not only because of the math and computation involved but also because of human factors. Technicians working on models tend to customize them as they go along, leaving broken trails or esoteric clues for those following them. Consequently, it is common for a model to be discontinued when one technician leaves the forecasting organization. It is important, then, that organizations be committed to modeling and that they cross-train personnel so that someone always knows how to use and update models.

SUMMARY

Once physicians identify treatment options, they typically offer patients some idea of the likelihood whether they will recover or, failing that, what their prospects are in the future. Policy analysts must offer the same service to decision makers. Politicians need to know what to expect from their policies. Again, policy analysts, like physicians, must prognosticate based on signs and symptoms placed in the context of the diagnosis and treatment strategy. And again, all information presented or available to analysts is not created equal. Different forecasting methods, employing varying degrees of data and information, often lead to different prognoses. Just as analysts must sort out signs and symptoms, competing hypotheses, and alternative treatments, so must they sort out good forecast information from bad. Generally, policy analysts evaluate the quality of the data used in forecasting, including its age, source, and reliability. They try to employ as many forecasting methods as possible to sort out biases endemic in different methodologies. They look for convergence among forecasts where possible, but on finding divergence, they tend to average forecasts, unless one is more compelling than the others. The key to forecasting for all analysts, including physicians, is identifying turning points—where trends get more or less favorable. The main caution always is not to believe that the future is a simple extrapolation from the past. In the policy arena, it mostly isn't.

CASE STUDY

Can Forecasting Target Industries for Development Strategies?

Most state and local governments husband their small economic development budgets by aiming at firms or industries perceived to have the greatest potential and turn to modelers to help them identify those targets (see also, Krikelas, 1992; Mills, 1993). The two most frequent targets are growth industries and industries or firms whose output is sold outside the region or whose output is a substitute for goods imported into the region.

These targets reflect important kernels of truth about economic development, but trying to find targets precise enough to shape state or local programs is an inappropriate use of forecasting models—the development process is too complex, and analytic techniques too imprecise (not to mention the undesirability of subsidizing one industry or sector at expense of another).

Most states and localities target industries that appear to have good prospects for growth either because the state and local resources are compatible with the industry's demands or because the industry has strong growth regionally or nationally (South Carolina Legislature, 1985). The South Carolina Legislature describes the typical targeting procedure:

> According to economic development specialists and practitioners, in deciding which industries to target, the [state] development agency must determine 1) the industries that are growing, 2) the growing industries' needs or location criteria, 3) the state's resources, and 4) the state's development goals. After this information is gathered, the development agency determines the growing industries whose location criteria most closely match the state's resources and development goals. The list of

specific targeted industry types should be updated as economic conditions and the state's needs change. (p. 2)

Tempting in theory, targeting cannot work in practice. Economic models cannot identify industries with any degree of precision; models and data are too crude, and matching industries with state resources is no indication which industries will respond to state programs. If it were possible to identify future growth industries through econometric techniques, then institutional investors, controlling vast portfolios, would be the first to employ them. But no empirical technique has yet proved sufficiently reliable. A cluster of target industries identified from economic statistics should not guide the deployment of state development resources.

Published data on what determines business growth and location are weak. Even at the state level, data are available for relatively few of the hundreds of relevant factors and for few of the different industries, accounting for less than half of employment and much less than half of net new jobs. Local data are even more meager. Even where industry-wide data are available for a local area, industry-wide generalizations—needed by industry recruiters—are often misleading because of the wide variations in production technologies or growth strategies among firms.

After an exhaustive attempt to identify growth industries for New York City, RAND Corporation researchers found none of their models, when applied retrospectively, was able to perform better than random selection (RAND Corporation, 1975). More recently, other researchers at the RAND Corporation found that there were some statistical indicators of sectors that were most likely to expand locally, including sectors with a smaller or larger share of local employment than of national employment and sectors (RAND Corporation, 1983). Their approach, however, works at a very high level of aggregation and does not identify industries that would be responsive to state and local development initiatives.

Even an accurate forecast of local growth industries would not predict how these industries would respond to public policies—a customized training program, a prepared site, tax abatements, or low-interest loans. There is no way of targeting a development strategy based on econometric analysis.

Forecasting is an imprecise science, yet is essential for policy analysts: Decision makers expect it. Most analysis of the consequences of alternative policies is prospective. There are a wide variety of techniques from which to choose, each with strengths and weaknesses that can be matched with the purpose of the forecast. Analysts should resist hiding bad ideas—such as targeting growth industries—under the apparent precision of economic modeling.

No one has yet invented a substitute for economic forecasting and no other discipline has established a better record. In fact, economists' record for identifying important factors that will shape the future is not as bad as their record for pointing out the best way to take advantage of them.

6

Evaluating

Much policy analysis consists of monitoring or evaluating existing programs. The failure of present programs or their unintended consequences are often at the root of new programs: environmental regulators with an angry queue of permit applicants, a technical college with graduates who remain without jobs, or a small business lending program that suffers high default rates.At the same time, successful programs offer useful analogies for new ways to deal with current problems: contracting out public services to promote efficiency and lower costs, providing incentives to managers to improve performance, or reducing recidivism rates among criminals.

Physicians monitor patients' condition to learn if prescribed treatments work. Monitoring is particularly important for unusual cases, for cases where the original diagnosis was uncertain, and for instances in which the patient gets worse. It is the only way to validate the original diagnosis, to check treatment effectiveness, to ensure patient compliance, and to improve physician diagnostic ability.

Systematic and impartial monitoring of public policy is rare. Agency efforts rarely probe deeply or provide basic information needed for good management (e.g., Barnekov & Hart, 1993; GAO, 1995; Weiwal et al., 1995). Policy analysts therefore monitor programs to avoid unpleasant surprises—projects and programs the poor performance of which leads the legislature to deny a budget request or shows up as a feature story in the press. Analysts must also conduct prospective evaluations to weigh different options. These tasks require different approaches: Monitoring requires the policy analyst to set up processes for acquiring regular and reliable measures of a program's performance; prospective evaluations require analysts to project possible costs and benefits of a program. Discussion of both follows.

Finally, policymakers need to evaluate the decision-making process itself. The decision maker must ensure that the staff solves problems smoothly—do they deal with important issues quickly and effectively? We describe this in a final section.

BOX 6.1

PERFORMANCE MEASURES

Output: What an organization produces or delivers, e.g., graduates from a college, welders trained, car titles completed, driver's licenses issued, trees planted, or people counseled.

Input: What an organization uses to produce or deliver a product or service, e.g., clients, patients, staff workers, supplies, buildings, equipment, and money.

Outcome: Whether what the organization produced or delivered had the intended consequence, that is, did the product or service do what it was supposed to do, e.g., people in training programs found jobs for which they were trained, received appropriate wages, and worked over the long term; people who completed remedial reading classes read at an appropriate level; or a technical assistance program for business reduced the failure rate.

RULE 1: MEASURE PROGRAM PERFORMANCE

We know a lot about public programs—expenditures on goods and services; numbers of people served; and, often, client characteristics and the amounts of goods or services consumed. But we rarely know what really matters: How well are the programs working?

It is more difficult to measure *outcomes* than *outputs* or inputs for many public programs. And there is less need for such measurements: Agency administrators do not face quarterly profit-and-loss statements and legislators do not always want to know whether their pet program succeeded. Therefore, decision makers monitor few programs regularly or systematically.

But measuring performance would allow program managers to determine what is going on: Is an experimental program worth *rolling out* statewide? Is a new appointed administrator doing well? Should next year's budget shift resources to other programs or to different local offices? In which local office are program clients served best?

Performance measures would be as invaluable to decision makers as to administrators. They could indicate which approaches solve problems most effectively: Are the long-term poor best helped to escape from welfare by workfare, remedial education, or subsidized placement programs? Which inner-city schools reduced dropout rates? Which helps new businesses more, financial aid or technical assistance?

And regular performance measures could identify problems before they appear in local newspapers. Elected officials can reduce the chance of embarrassing problems that divert attention from their policy agenda by checking regularly on how well programs serve clients.

But most important, performance measures help the people the program is intended to serve. If displaced workers know how well training programs placed graduates in jobs, they will be able to make informed choices about what new careers to pursue. An educated consumer, free to choose among programs, is the strongest enforcer of *accountability*.

To many people in public office, the allegation that programs are not held accountable may seem strange. If they are not, to what end are the reams of paper filed to justify the tiniest expenditure, promotion, or hiring? But accounting is not accountability. All public administrators must file seemingly endless reports to show that public money was spent as intended by numbers of participants, numbers requiring special attention, hours spent in class, qualifications of teachers, and curricula used. Teachers often spend more time writing than do their students to account for each hour in the classroom. "So much of what we call management," said Peter Drucker (1964), "consists in making it difficult for people to work" (p. 6).

Spending money legally does not mean it has been spent effectively. Few states compile data to demonstrate whether students learn, how much students learn, or whether what they have learned helped them land a job or pursue further studies.

We hold programs accountable by judging whether their activities follow the procedures laid out in volumes of regulatory small print. We rarely ask whether the outcomes indicate that people are better off for having participated.

Collecting performance data must be the central function of program managers—not something undertaken when demanded by legislative auditors or state or federal funding sources. Extensive databases that agencies already maintain and the data-processing power of portable computers make it possible for all programs to develop and manage information systems useful to managers, policymakers, and clients.

No one would argue that measuring performance is easy or even that it can be done perfectly. Few people would even claim that measuring performance will be popular. But without systematic performance measurement, we can never learn from experience.

The wrong measure of performance can be—and has been—more harmful than no measure at all. Most program administrators will do whatever they can to generate good numbers, especially if they believe it may earn them a larger budget next year or recognition from the community they serve.

BOX 6.2

GOALS AND OBJECTIVES DEFINED

Goal: A general statement concerning what an organization would like to achieve at some future time, e.g, reduce poverty in a region, teach children to read, or train workers as welders.

Objective: A specific statement laying out quantitative measures to ascertain whether a goal was achieved, e.g., the number of persons whose income falls below federal poverty guidelines will be reduced by 50% over the next 12 months; 400 children in high school now reading at a 1st-grade level will score at or above a 12th-grade reading level on the state's reading proficiency test in X years; or 50% of welders enrolled in the local vocational school will pass the state's licensing test for welders at the completion of their 6-month course of study.

But without performance measures, managers manage blindly, policy-makers have no idea what works, and clients are clueless about where they may be best served. To create an effective performance measurement system, policymakers need to answer four questions:

1. Are the program goals stated clearly? What group of people is the program intended to serve, and how does the program intend to serve them?

2. How can progress toward these goals best be measured? What variables best measure how well these goals have been achieved? What data sources can be employed to provide regular reports at a reasonable cost?

3. How can incentives be linked to goal attainment? Will managers improve performance if agencies receive flexible, discretionary funds when goals are attained?

4. Who will object to performance measures and how can their objections be met? No one likes being measured, especially if he or she also feels underpaid and overworked. What is the best way to deal with opposition?

RULE 2: STATE PROGRAM GOALS CLEARLY

Although program goals are usually stated in the preamble to the ena-bling legislation or in a press release from officials announcing the pro-gram's creation, these statements often confuse as much as they clarify. The first task in creating a performance measurement system is to develop a working statement of consistent program goals.

By the time a program has gained the legislative or executive support needed to give it life, its original straightforward objectives have usually become confused. Interested people transform it to serve populations and functions its original sponsors never intended. Compromise is how political decisions are made.

Public programs become "like Caesar's wife—all things to all people," in the words of the Chicago politician. For example, one state identified its strategic economic development goal as "full employment for the state [undefined], with a job that pays a living wage to every person who wants or needs to work, and a workforce which meets the current and future needs of employers." This ambitious goal was disaggregated into 24 specific objectives, listed without priorities. Because of the relatively small influence of state programs when compared to shifts in overall economic conditions, this goal statement provides little direct guidance to those who would try to measure the strategy's effectiveness. What are realistic goals for the strategy, and what priorities should they enjoy?

Even if focused, goals may be mutually inconsistent. One state development program faced the dual goals of "new job creation" and "the adoption of high-technology means of production." Yet, new technologies often save labor. In the event of a conflict, which goal should take priority? Or consider state enterprise zone programs. States created zones to attract employers to distressed areas to create jobs for poor people. Yet, states offered employers capital incentives the effect of which was to make them more dependent on machines and less on labor.

Many public programs capture a clientele large enough to build legislative support but often far too large for dedicated program resources. A training program in one state, budgeted at less than $2 million, helps displaced farmers, displaced homemakers, and high school dropouts. In measuring performance, what weight should be given to the different groups?

There is no easy way to answer these questions. But in trying to resolve them, policymakers will provide valuable management information to program managers. And if you really want it done, make your request clearly.

RULE 3: DEVELOP YARDSTICKS
FOR MEASURING PROGRESS

Public programs aim at a wide variety of objectives, from reducing pregnancies among teenagers in school to training dislocated workers, helping drug addicts, creating jobs, and placing welfare recipients in unsubsidized work. Performance with respect to these goals can never be measured perfectly, but, for almost all goals, information can be developed to give approximate measures. Measuring against a standard—such as programs in other states or competing programs in a state—policy analysts refer to as *benchmarking*.

For example, many programs concern what happens to people when they enter the labor market. States already track labor market experience through unemployment insurance (UI) systems. To determine eligibility for UI, states monitor employment and earnings of all working people, identifying people through their Social Security numbers. Although individual data cannot be disclosed, files can be used to determine the work experience of those passing through a program.

For example, Arizona experimented with publication of placement rates and earnings of classes graduating from postsecondary training programs. The program was used for one year—before state funding was cut off in the confusion preceding the impeachment of Governor Evan Meachem in 1987. Every postsecondary institution in the state supplied a list of graduates' Social Security numbers, which were compared with UI records by the Department of Economic Security. A special center, set up at Northern Arizona University, determined how to deal with data problems and compiled a report showing average placement rates and earnings for every class in every institution with more than 25 completers. Although no attempt was made to follow graduates out of state, over 90% of the graduates showed up on the state's files.

The program's cost was low—the state's Department of Economic Security marshaled existing resources to match and felt that the data were a useful addition to the economic indicators that the department already published.

These data are far more reliable than attempts to contact graduates by mail or telephone, the basis for most placement statistics reported by vocational institutions, with fewer than 15% of the class contacted. It is much simpler for schools to submit Social Security numbers than to try to contact students themselves.

When designing performance measures, it is always tempting to make them as comprehensive as possible. Most attempts to determine what happens to people graduating from training programs, for example, tried to discover whether graduates use the new skills they acquired in the program. But this requires matching curriculum descriptions with one of the 1,100 occupational classifications defined by the Bureau of Labor Statistics. At a time when technology is transforming occupations, this is a futile quest. Even with 1,100 occupations specified, the skills clustered within each make it almost impossible to match job requirements with training skills: Lion tamers and veterinarians are in the same category!

The value placed on graduates' qualifications is best measured by how much their employers are willing to pay them and how long they stay on the job. For example, as financial institutions adapted their operations to the power of the computer, they hired more and more computer programmers and operators. Yet, several shunned federally trained computer experts in favor of people with strong communications skills. They reasoned that they can more easily teach computer programming on the job than the ability to communicate. This does not mean that communications graduates were not appropriate to the job or that their training was irrelevant.

RULE 4: CREATE INCENTIVES
FOR GOOD PERFORMANCE

Never tell people how to do things. Tell them what you want them to achieve and they surprise you with their ingenuity.
—General George S. Patton, *The Patton Papers* (1974)

Measuring performance is the first step toward encouraging better performance. It can help decision makers determine funding allocation effectiveness, and it can help departmental administrators determine whether they are getting the intended results and whether all local offices are performing at equal effectiveness.

But decision makers must be aware that the simple act of measuring the performance of public programs changes the way programs are run. As soon as administrators' behavior is measured, they will explore ways to improve their test scores in hopes that they will earn a higher budget or larger staff. Therein lays one of the potential pitfalls of performance measurement: In redeploying resources to meet measured objectives, agencies are likely to cut back on how well they meet nonmeasured objectives.

Activities funded under the federal Job Training Partnership Act (JTPA) are good examples. The system pioneered rigorous performance standards, but, by setting, as principal goal, a low cost per placement, JTPA discouraged local agencies from serving the hardest to employ or from providing clients with in-depth education and training. Under JTPA's predecessor, the Comprehensive Employment and Training Act (CETA), only 11% of all those served were offered placement assistance, the lowest-cost type of activity. Under JTPA, 34% receive help in finding work but no classroom training or remedial education.

The only way to avoid these undesirable outcomes is to *game* agency behavior when selecting performance measures. Consider whether actions of a hard-pressed manager in pursuit of the measured objectives might jeopardize unmeasured ones. For example, JTPA decision makers could have anticipated *creaming* and created incentives to serve the hard to place: GED or increases in reading level could be counted as desirable outcomes, or placement costs for people unable to read at the 7th-grade level could be discounted. Most important, quarterly results could be monitored to determine whether the right mix of people were served.

An obvious incentive is to tie the distribution of funds among local agencies to how well they perform according to measured indicators—a step under exploration by a growing number of states and communities. For example, no states now tie distribution of vocational funding to placement rates, but 17 collect placement rate data for program evaluation purposes only. Florida, for example, requires vocational programs to meet a 70% placement target. If they fail, they go on probation and receive peer assistance. If there is no improvement after 3 years, state funds are terminated.

Several states offer schools financial incentives for raising test scores and reducing dropout rates. Rewards result from increasing test scores, not for overall level of test scores, to avoid penalizing schools with large numbers of disadvantaged students or small budgets: Nationwide, under school reform, some of the poorest schools are capable of the greatest improvements in performance. Performance measures need not favor the already successful or well endowed.

Another, and even more controversial incentive, allows program clients greater choice in selecting the agencies serving them. People enrolling in education or training, for example, enjoy some flexibility in program choice. Information on past placement rates and graduate earnings would help them make more informed decisions.

RULE 5: ANTICIPATE OPPOSITION

Not surprisingly, those whose performance is to be measured do not always welcome the prospect. As evidence of this, the GAO discovered that few agencies in 1997 had adequately implemented the 1993 Government Performance Act, the flagship of federal reinventing government initiatives (Barr, 1997). Some of their objections are understandable and must be accommodated. But some opposition is simply natural resistance to change.

Fear 1. We are doing the best we can with limited resources

All people like to believe that they are doing the best job possible. Most are. But could someone else do our job more effectively? Measuring performance will appear to reflect dissatisfaction with present management practices. But the need to measure does not reflect a belief that some managers are not exerting as much effort as others. It does, however, provide a way of finding out the suitability of all those appointed to command.

Potential resistance to performance measurement is illustrated by what happened when a western state attempted to measure how well its sheltered workshops performed in finding private jobs for developmentally disabled clients. A consultant designed a simple management information system that showed monthly, for each workshop, the percentage of revenues that was privately generated—a report distributed throughout the system and used by counties when contracting with nonprofit organizations for sheltered workshops for the developmentally disabled.

Poorly performing workshops—often those in business a long time and with a "business as usual approach" to service delivery—quite naturally opposed the system. They marshaled political influence to open a legislative investigation and audit of the consultant. They argued that their responsibilities were far broader than simply securing private contracts and succeeded eventually in having the system suspended, despite strong support for the idea from smaller, innovative workshops, which attracted a much larger share of private funds.

Performance measures are no substitute for managerial skills in those running programs. Managers should be able to make sensible exceptions to general rules. But to make sensible exceptions, the manager needs regular data on what is going on. Hard work and stress are not a sign that better performance is impossible.

Fear 2. Performance measures do not reflect the value of the program

Public administrators also oppose performance measurement on the grounds that it oversimplifies their complex day-to-day responsibilities: Can a teacher's job be reduced to improving student test scores, lowering dropout rates, or increasing the enthusiasm with which students find work?

The answer is clearly no. But effective teachers will fare better on these outcomes. Yet, because of powerful lobbying by teachers and school administrators, the first rounds of education reform concentrated on raising teacher pay and qualifications and reducing class sizes. Policymakers devoted much less effort to developing performance-based funding systems or merit pay systems.

Several states acceded to pressures against performance measures and relaxed graduation requirements and stringent outcome measures. The Texas legislature eliminated the subject knowledge section of its teacher competency exams; the Alabama legislature abandoned its teacher career ladder; the Missouri legislature considered a bill barring release to the public of student achievement scores; a panel of superintendents and principals appointed by the governor of South Dakota urged that regulations governing school accreditation be weakened and that South Dakota's new, tougher high school graduation requirement be eliminated (Bennett, 1988).

Fear 3. The data will be inaccurate

Opponents also argue, with some justification, that performance measurement is inaccurate. Graduate vocational program placement rates are often compiled through a mail survey conducted by the school several months after graduation. A return rate of below 15% is not unusual, and is not likely to be representative of the entire class: Those unable to find work may be hard to reach or unwilling to fill out the questionnaire. A school district in Indiana would have been penalized under that state's new accreditation procedures because it scheduled classes for teenage mothers for 3 1/2 days a week—an exemplary program that led to a high measured absentee rate.

Some opposition to performance measures is reasonable. The measures are, after all, imperfect. Therefore, it is important to create a system that ensures a fair hearing for opponents and those who will use it. In Arizona, for example, the act mandating the measurement of placement rates created a center at Northern Arizona University with a board composed of vocational technology directors, state officials, and university faculty to determine what counted as a placement and how to deal with data problems. The resulting system was more readily accepted and more widely used.

Fear 4. Performance measurement will lead to creaming

Managers of human service programs naturally fear that measuring performance will lead to *creaming*. To raise placement rates or to increase clients served, managers will pick those who will graduate most quickly or find work easily. Although the tendency to cream is inevitable, it can be countered. By specifying carefully who the program is meant to serve or by making specific allowance for the difficulty of serving certain clients, creaming can be contained.

Fear 5. We are too regulated to do things any better

Managers resent performance evaluation if they or their staff have little discretionary power to shape their own success. When welfare caseworkers must comply with detailed rules and regulations, they may have little time to find jobs for their clients. If teachers must follow a cumbersome curriculum hour by hour, they have little leeway to develop more innovative ways to teach. Most states tried to regulate excellence into existence. They forgot about the need to delegate to competent subordinates and let them get on with their work.

Measuring performance makes sense only if day-to-day management is *decentralized.* The purpose is to judge how well programs perform, not how well they conform. Giving local administrators greater discretion encourages experimentation. Some experiments will succeed, some will not. Without experimentation, agencies will slowly become dominated by mediocre programs and staff.

The trade-offs between reduced state oversight of operations in exchange for greater local accountability for results were summarized neatly by Governor Lamar Alexander of Tennessee in 1986. In a news conference stating the position of the 50 governors toward improving the quality of education, he offered, "We'll regulate less, if schools and school districts will perform better."

Performance reporting systems are the way large private firms manage while still leaving employees the incentive and capacity to innovate.

Fear 6. No one will use these data anyway

Gimmicks to improve public management are not new (Micklewait & Wooldridge, 1996). Zero-based budgeting and performance-based budget systems enjoyed brief popularity among experts in public administration. Most local administrators worked in agencies long enough to remember several previous attempts to improve efficiency. When Governor Bob Graham's staff first introduced the idea of performance measurement, they were opposed by many bureaucrats who had invested many person-hours under previous administrations filling out forms, the results of which were never reflected in agency budgets.

This fear is understandable. Any system of performance measurement inevitably carries bad as well as good news to the administration. Some programs and some local offices will not show up well. Since the press will have access to quarterly reports, and since most reporters have a bias toward reporting bad news, administrations will be tempted to portray numbers depicting good news. If they do, then the system fails to serve its purpose. Introducing performance measures therefore must be done gradually. As each step is introduced, information must be linked to rewards and sanctions associated with good performance. Governor Graham increased, each year, the number of agencies and programs for which performance targets were set. The governor and staff members analyzed and discussed quarterly reports with administrators. In this way, the chief executive gained credibility for his performance program.

RULE 6: EVALUATE THE EVALUATORS

But . . . let us not overestimate the importance of the economic problem, or sacrifice to its supposed necessities other matters of greater and more permanent significance. It should be matter for specialists—like dentistry. If economists could manage to get themselves thought of as humble, competent people, on a level with dentists, that would be splendid.

John Maynard Keynes, *Essays in Persuasion* (1933)

Monitoring should apply to the policy process as well as to policies. It is important to know how well the decision maker's staff perform: Are the right data being collected? Are diagnoses being made well? Are a broad spectrum of treatment options being investigated? Are important issues missed? Are the decision maker's priorities reflected in the level of effort accorded to different issues?

Every issue passing through the policy office (or its equivalent) of elected or appointed officials at all levels should be tracked on an *issue treatment file*. This format is the key tool in monitoring policy staff's work. It is also useful to academic policy researchers who want to provide decision makers with information in a format most useful to them.

SUMMARY

In the past few years, government and medicine have gone a major transition—evaluating policy and patients using outcome measures against an established set of goals and objectives rather than measuring inputs and outcomes. In medicine, physicians establish a patient management strategy to guide treatment, then evaluate whether or not the treatment did what was intended—restore health, improve quality of life, reduce pain, or extend life. Likewise, policy analysts must be concerned with how well policy interventions worked, not with how much money or resources were expended as input and how much was produced as output. For evaluation to be effective, it must be built into all programs or policies; it must be widely accepted by decision makers, policymakers, and subordinate staff; and it must be measurable, with performance results widely reported. When evaluation is undertaken, decision makers must take care to monitor the evaluators as well as programs and policies evaluated.

CASE STUDIES

Case 1. Measuring Policy Outcomes in Oregon and Minnesota

Two states, Oregon and Minnesota, over a decade ago started setting specific measurable targets for their state and carefully monitoring progress. They set in motion this approach, now used widely in other states.

Oregon's benchmarks grew out of the strategic vision for the state. The Oregon Progress Board, a group of public and private community leaders, developed the first benchmarks. Benchmarks were developed through 12 statewide meetings and with detailed written comments from over 200 groups and organizations. They were based on the premise that "Oregon will have the best chance of achieving an attractive future if Oregonians agree clearly on where we want to go and then join together to accomplish those goals" (Oregon Progress Board, 1982).

The board recommendations were eventually approved by the legislature. They included a total of 160 benchmarks measuring how the state was performing with respect to three goals: exceptional individuals, outstanding quality of life, and a robust diversified economy. Seventeen of the measures were identified as short-term lead benchmarks, related to urgent problems in which the board wanted to see progress within 5 years, such as reducing the rate of teen pregnancies, enrolling people in vocational programs, expanding access to basic health care, and cutting workers' compensation costs.

A further 13 benchmarks were listed as key—fundamental, enduring measures of Oregon's vitality and health. These included improving basic student skills, reducing the crime rate, and raising Oregon's per capita income as a percentage of the U.S. average.

Minnesota Milestones was set up to correspond with Oregon's program. The draft report was prepared not by a separate organization as in Oregon but by the state's Planning Office. In dozens of discussion groups around the state, citizens expressed their vision of the future—a caring community; the natural environment sustained; an efficient and fair economy; creative citizens; and a responsive, efficient government. Twenty-seven goals were engaged, everything from "Our children shall not live in poverty" to "Government will be more efficient" and 103 specific measures were identified and matched with each goal from "reducing to 3 percent by the year 2020 the percent of children living in poverty" to "holding the number of state and local government employees per 10,000 population to 480" (State Planning Office, 1983). Thousands of copies of the draft were mailed, complete with a mail-in questionnaire.

Case 2. Florida's Policy Accountability System

Although governors are responsible for setting policy for state agencies, most have little systematic information that tells them whether their policies are being carried out or whether the gubernatorial appointments are managing their agencies well. As a result, well-intentioned strategies stall and the morning newspaper can bring unpleasant stories of agency incompetence or worse.

Under Governor Bob Graham, Florida established an accountability system allowing the governor's office staff to monitor how well agencies were performing and to encourage agencies to improve performance. Goals were set for each agency and reviewed with agency heads quarterly. The system assumes that the budget is the governor's single most important resource for policy implementation. The accountability system was made possible by moving the state planning and budgeting functions out of the Department of Administration and into the Executive Office of the Governor.

The first step was to develop clearly stated policy priorities covering all major policy areas. Agencies had to translate these broad priorities into specific, measurable targets for their programs. As part of the 1981 budgetary process, agencies designed budget-related program performance measures to accompany budget requests. The results were mixed because agency staff resisted the order. They weren't familiar with management information systems and until that year there had been no clearly articulated policies to provide a baseline for setting measurable objectives. Many program professionals and managers saw quantitative outcome measures as threats to their professional authority, their freedom to maneuver, and the agencies' integrity. And agency staff could remember previous attempts at scientific management, used by executive or legislative decision makers.

Therefore, Governor Graham requested the Office of Planning and Budgeting to *negotiate* a set of performance agreements with each agency. These negotiations were limited to those programs that were related to the governor's top priorities—about 5% of all agency program activities.

In the first year of the process, most negotiated measures were not unlike the workload measures previously used by the agency. By the second year, about one half of the participating agencies developed solid outcome-oriented performance agreement measures in their high-priority program areas. Finally, in the third year, over two thirds of all measures approved by the governor could be used to assess agency effectiveness with reasonable accuracy.

7

Figuring Out What to Say

A man is not necessarily intelligent because he has plenty of ideas
any more than he is a good general because
he has plenty of soldiers.

—Sebastien Chamfort, *Maximes par Chamfort* (1805/1966)

When analysts try to summarize what they know, they face a dilemma. Their work, we hope, embodies a lot of data and complex techniques—although, perhaps, not as much data or as sophisticated techniques as they would have others believe. Few elected or appointed officials who must make final decisions will understand all that has gone into the policy analyst's work. After all, that's why they use experts.

But how can analysts communicate nuances of their research in a way that decision makers can use? First, they must simplify, but without omitting important, and often ambiguous, findings. Decision makers cannot plow through reams of detail, but they don't want to be given a false sense of security in the recommendations they will make. Decision makers have too much material crossing their desks to spend as much time as the analyst would like them to on the subtleties of information available. The analyst must act as both writer and editor—ready to provide further information if certain issues emerge as critical in building the consensus needed to move a measure through the tortuous legislative or bureaucratic processes. Alain Enthoven (1974), advisor to the Secretary of Defense during the 1960s, gave good advice: "Usually recommendations are less valuable and less interesting than the content of the analysis; the way the problem is posed, the alternatives invented or designed, the data collected and evaluated, the criteria used. . . . The best analyses highlight which assumptions, initial judgments and valuations lead to which conclusions and how" (p. 25).

There are seven rules analysts can follow to help decide what decision makers absolutely need to know and what can be left out.

RULE 1: ANALYZE POLICY, NOT POLITICS

> *Economic problems have no sharp edges; they shade off*
> *imperceptibly into politics, sociology, and ethics. Indeed,*
> *it is hardly an exaggeration to say that the ultimate answer*
> *to every economic problem lies in some other field.*
> —Kenneth Boulding, *The Impact of the Social Sciences* (1966b, p. 56)

Analysts should describe what they know about policies under consideration but avoid discussing politics. However tempting, avoid musing about how the public will react to alternative proposals or how a policy should be marketed. It will inevitably come back to haunt you. Policy, not politics, is an analyst's area of strength. Policy analysts did not run for office. The decision maker has either run for office or is, at least, accustomed to acting in the public's eye. Decision makers are sensitive to the public's views or, at least, are directly accountable to them.

Decision makers sometimes ask analysts for their opinions or recommendations, but this is a secondary role, distinct from objectively diagnosing problems and examining alternative prescriptions. Analysts should enter the political arena with extreme care. Their expertise lies elsewhere. When Leon Keyserling, chairman of President Truman's Council of Economic Advisors, recommended an action to the president on the grounds that it would be good politics, he was told, "Don't try to teach your grandmother to suck eggs" (Verdier, 1984, p. 424). Policy analysts must recognize that their clients make decisions based on many considerations, of which technical analysis is only a part. If decisions appear to fly in the face of analysis, they need not devalue either analyst or analysis. The best word of advice for policy analysts is not to take things personally.

The relationship between expert and decision maker builds slowly. After all, most decision makers lack the technical expertise to judge how good experts are at their jobs (Hamilton, 1992), just as most technicians know little of the political context within which decisions will be taken. Decision makers find ways to test the values and instincts of would-be expert advisors. These tests are very different from the academic rules against which many experts are used to being judged. Decision makers want to know whether expert advice is practical and plausible: Remember, decision makers need to be able to communicate the basis of their decisions to their constituents, if they are elected, or to their staff, if they are appointed. Is the expert respectable or on the fringe (Hamilton, 1992)? If the expert does not have a strong following among his or her professional associates, his or her reputation could undermine the program—however sound the analysis. Are the expert's values compatible with those of the decision maker? Experts often overemphasize their own "scientific objectivity"—many decision makers know experts often have hidden axes to grind or political agendas of their own.

Apparently irrelevant questions posed by decision makers are often intended to gather these collateral data. Experts who reveal themselves as insensitive to values or constituents dear to the decision maker or ignorant of institutional realities will find it increasingly difficult to penetrate the decision-making process. Often, they will not be told that their advice has fallen short of decision makers' expectations—those involved in politics rarely want to burn bridges unless they really have to.

Trust between expert and decision maker therefore builds through informal testing. An expert's ideas permeate the policy arena gradually—particularly if those ideas are innovative and their sponsors unknown. Decision makers who publicly support a genuinely innovative approach risk loss of power and influence. They usually wait while ideas are tested in the public arena. The expert often feels that the decision maker, so supportive in a one-on-one meeting, has deserted the issue now that it has been debated in public.

But decision makers often need *deniability*—the ability to say that they were never "100% behind the program." They wait while the issue is subject to strenuous opposition. What sort of opposition does the idea draw? Are hidden flaws revealed? A onetime speaker of the Texas legislature compared the process to running sacred cows up a flagpole to see which draw fire. Anyone advocating new ideas must expect them to pass through this testing process—although they will rarely be told what the rules are or even when a final decision has been taken. But don't carry deniability too far at the risk of losing credibility (see Clines, 1998)

When decision makers come to trust experts, they will ask them for recommendations. But the advisory role grows out of and does not precede the role as explainer.

RULE 2: KEEP IT SIMPLE

It is all right for experts to think like social scientists, but they shouldn't sound like them if they want nonscientists to listen. Decision makers rightly view the product of complex models with suspicion. They know that experts can be hired to arrive at any conclusion. Complex analyses are essential for some tasks: predicting fiscal consequences of tax changes, increases in welfare benefits, or changes in education finance formulas. But mathematical models inevitably omit many aspects of the real world that decision makers feel are important. The manipulation of complex models may help us arrive at policy conclusions. The military offers a simple maxim: "Keep it simple, stupid," or KISS, for short.

It is better to be roughly right by applying common sense than exactly wrong by applying complex models. When not trapped by data-driven models, social scientists may be trapped by the logical demands of their theories and forget to ask whether theories help us understand observable life. Theory, after all, can be an organized way of going wrong with confidence.

Herbert Stein has said, "Most of the economics that is usable for advising on public policy is at about the level of the introductory undergraduate course. . . . Economists do not know very much; other people, including the politicians who make economic policy, know even less about economics than economists do" (as quoted in Hamilton, 1992, p. 62).

Economists have several valuable tools for policy analysis, but they are often difficult to explain. Sometimes, a carefully designed analogy can help convey a complex point forcefully. The economist Ed Kane was one of the few people to predict the savings and loan debacle. Describing how politicians could allow the problem to escalate to a $200 billion bailout, he wrote,

> Elected politicians have behaved like members of a dinner party who lack the funds to pay the check that the restaurateur has placed before them. Rather than negotiating with the restaurateur to develop a workable payment plan, they have stayed at their table for an uncomfortably long time and even ordered an unwanted round or two of after dinner drinks. As they sip those drinks, some of the diners may content themselves with hoping that a lottery ticket they have in their pockets will miraculously cure their growing debt. (1989, p. 34)

Opportunity Cost. The notion that costs associated with one course of action are the most valuable alternative uses of resources employed (including the time of decision makers) often conflicts with the intuitive notion equating costs with budgetary expenditures. Items that do not show up on the budget—foregone value of timber that could be harvested on federal or state land, for example—are real costs. The economists Christopher Leman and Robert Nelson (1981) observe, "The huge inventories of virgin timber held by the U.S. Forest Service represent a capital investment with a high opportunity cost, but one seldom taken into account in timber management decisions" (p. 98). Overlooking opportunity costs notoriously encourages us to be generous with other people's money (Rhoads, 1978, p. 8):

> Some years ago a poll found overwhelming support for increased spending on social programs. . . . But when the same people were asked if more should be spent even if more tax money were required, those favorably disposed fell to 34 percent. . . . We, the public, seem quite willing, if given half a chance, to believe that there is such a thing as a free lunch.
>
> Despite administrators' and legislators' greater knowledge of public affairs, their neglect of opportunity costs is not surprising. . . . It is not only natural but in most ways advantageous, to have administrators who care more about their programs than the average citizen does. [But] opportunity costs do not go away just because some people stop thinking of them. It is more difficult to give them due weight when they do not appear in the sitting legislature's budget.

Marginalism. Comparison of incremental changes in total costs and benefits that can be traced to specific policies often conflicts with the decision maker's desire to attribute all events that follow project implementation to that policy. For example, many decision makers count as the benefits of a public loan to an ailing business all the jobs retained in that business. They may even inflate those numbers by adding jobs "created" through the *multiplier effect* of spending the retained payrolls in the community. When all the events occurring after an action are attributed to that action, it is very easy to demonstrate a high rate of return.

Consumption Versus Investment. The distinction between actions yielding immediate benefits and those the benefits of which will be enjoyed over a longer time period is important. Programs that prevent people from becoming dependent on welfare—by keeping potential dropouts in high school, for example—cannot be compared directly to the operating costs of the Department of Motor Vehicles.

Unintended Consequences. Economists are keenly aware how people change their behavior when the complex array of incentives they face is changed. They know that there are many ways in which a well-intentioned policy may backfire.

Value. Economists argue that values are subjective—measured by what people are prepared to pay—not inherent. If people buy pet rocks, what they paid measures how much they valued their rocks. You may see the rocks as a waste of money. But decision makers must wrestle with many goods and activities the market value of which the public refuses to accept: dog fighting and child pornography, for example. We often impose values through the political process. Therefore, analysts should be explicit about values embodied in their analysis.

Many noneconomists retain notions that value is linked to the cost of production. This attempt to derive an objective source of value confused economists for centuries—Adam Smith failed to arrive at a satisfactory definition of value, and Karl Marx attributed value to the amount of labor expended to produce goods. Against these theories, the economist's concept of subjective value is important and useful.

Useful as these tools are to the expert, experts should keep theoretical discussions to themselves.

Because social science insights are not intuitively obvious, academics must explain analyses carefully, but should not use the opportunity to explain their discipline. John Brandl (1985), a veteran member of the Minnesota legislature (and a Humphrey Institute professor), argues that by making general assertions, economists "try to persuade policy-makers to adopt key assumptions of economic theory—a particular understanding of self-interest, for example, or the contention that a government has preferences and responds as would an individual. . . . However, legislators perceive these proposals as statistical and abstract or the economists as advocates of a particular proposal rather than as disinterested forecasters of policy effects" (p. 347).

RULE 3: COMMUNICATE REASONING
AS WELL AS BOTTOM LINES

> *When my colleagues at the New York Times use the word*
> *"academic" they intend no compliment; they mean irrelevant. And*
> *when my former colleagues in the academy describe someone's*
> *work as "journalistic," they mean shallow.*
> —Michael Weinstein, "Editorial Notebook," *New York Times (1990, p. A25)*

Although social scientists are fond of stressing their disciplines' scientific objectivity, their conclusions depend heavily on the assumptions made, the theoretical constructs used, and their own bias. Social science is not and cannot be value free. Therefore, the economic or social model used successfully in policy analysis should be described to decision makers and the public, in simple terms. Since patients cannot easily judge the efficacy of doctors' techniques, Western patients tend to rely on doctors whose techniques, they feel, "express so-called scientific principles which are widely accepted if not intelligently appreciated" (Miller, 1978, p. 86). If patients do not accept the rationale on which the physician's authority rests, they turn away. If voters do not accept a politician's rationale, they also turn away. A political leader will neither win the support of the legislature nor receive credit from the public for his or her policies unless he or she communicates the strategy's underlying rationale.

Policy statements need not be economics seminars but should contain relevant aspects of the model in statements about problem causes and reasons for selecting the proposed approach for dealing with it, in order to inspire public confidence that the remedy may work. Congressman Lee H. Hamilton (1992), a veteran of hundreds of public hearings, suggests, "Policy-makers need help in getting the economics right, even when only elementary principles are involved. It is important to spell out where the economy stands and where it is projected to go, what is right and wrong about the situation, the options for changes, and the risks and advantages of my recommended course of action" (p. 62).

There are many examples of leaders winning election and reelection based on their own charismatic power to persuade people of their capacity as a "healer" without divulging the scientific framework on which their powers rest. This is, however, a rare feat, often beyond leaders wrestling with economic issues today. President Reagan explained *supply side economics* as part of his 1980 election campaign with the result that he was able to pass his extensive legislative agenda during his first 2 years in office.

An example of the successful communication of a new economic model was the campaign for educational reform waged in Mississippi early in the 1980s. Mississippi had invented the traditional approach to the development and use of industrial revenue bonds and tax abatements in the mid-1930s with its Balance Agriculture With Industry program. Although firms had taken advantage of the incentives for nearly half a century, in 1980, the state still ranked last with respect to most measures of development. William Winter campaigned for governor on a platform of education reform—compulsory kindergarten and higher qualifications and pay for teachers paid for through higher taxes. But the thrust of reform was that measures were needed to stimulate economic development. He wanted to replace the old incentive model with one that more fully encompassed human capital. The first attempt to introduce legislation failed.

Communication of Winter's new model of development was then inten-
sified. During the 18 months between inauguration and the second (and
successful) introduction of the legislation, the governor and his senior
cabinet made over 500 speeches on the link between education and economic development. Stark statistics of the state's economic predicament
and its poorly educated workforce were easily absorbed and repeated by
the media. On December 21, 1982, Governor Winter signed the education
reform package.

RULE 4: USE NUMBERS SPARINGLY

*The very power of the computer to simulate complex systems by
very high-speed arithmetic may prevent search for those simplified
formulations which are the essence of progress.*
—Kenneth Boulding, *Economic Analysis* (1966a, p. 42)

Numbers are a useful way to illustrate a point, but are rarely decisive.
Many academics may regard the final result of a data run as the basis of
reportable and publishable research. Decision makers will be more cautious. For them, numbers are a way of illustrating a plausible argument—
not the argument itself.

A few well-chosen facts are more effective than layers of computer
printout, but must be derived from sound and comprehensible analysis.
James Verdier (1984) describes how Secretary of the Treasury Joseph Barr,
in 1969, provoked Congress into reforming income taxes by pointing out
that 21 people who earned more than $1 million in 1967 paid no taxes.
Robert McIntire of Citizens for Tax Justice played the same role in the 1986
Tax Act by listing *Fortune* 500 companies that paid no federal taxes.

By collecting and analyzing economic statistics, economists can give
decision makers more precise, or even new, ways of looking at public
policy issues. But facts should never be more than a means to an end. They
allow us to explore the issue—the better the facts, the more effective our
exploration. Be sure to interpret data and present them in a way that
politicians can use in speeches to the general public. If you don't, others
will. For example, the average high school graduate has watched 18,000
hours of TV. But 18,000 is a large number that few of us appreciate.
Describing television viewing habits of children as "more hours than

children spend in classrooms between kindergarten and high school graduation" makes the reader aware immediately of the size of the number and the point of citing it.

Most experts will be uncomfortable with the appearance of analysis by anecdote. It seems unscientific. But the good analyst uses anecdotes to illustrate, not to reason. Undigested data can sometimes be less effective than no data at all. Higher-level governments fudge together data that looks very different from the perspective of local communities. The data won't enervate elected officials who represent much smaller constituencies. Issues may not be real to them until they understand what the data mean for their district. If local data are not available, local examples should be used as illustrations—a new business, an education program, or a waste disposal problem, for example.

Although you use aggregate data in your analysis, use specific cases, wherever possible, to illustrate your conclusions. Concrete examples condition how people think about issues. Most of us lack the habit of conceptual thought and think about issues in terms of real instances. Elected leaders worry about the particular problems their constituents face because they must help their constituents. Unless they can visualize problems in the same way their constituents talk about them, politicians may be unable to picture why one approach may be better than others. President Clinton personalizes his policies by asking people directly affected by them to appear with him at news conferences, speeches, or announcements. When proposing billions in grants and incentives for child care, President Clinton entered his news conference in the company of children in day care (Seelye, 1998).

If you do not describe the data and their implications clearly, the press is prone to getting the wrong story—even if it gets the facts right. During the late 1980s, when the inflation had fallen to a long-time low of 1.5% a year, *The New York Times* regularly reported that the Consumer Price Index had reached record levels. The real story was the very low rate of price change, not its overall level.

RULE 5: ELUCIDATE, DON'T ADVOCATE

It is not the province of the Political Economist to advise—
he is there to tell you how you may become rich, but he is not to
advise you to prefer riches to indolence, or indolence to riches.
—David Ricardo, *On the Principles of Political Economy* (1819)

Analysts advocating particular policies risk losing the trust of decision makers. When we feel a strong urge to advocate, we should step back and review the limits of what we know about the decision in question. Our professional training allows us to understand aspects of the question, but not all of it. Much remains buried in the political process that technical skills cannot unearth. The British economist Alec Cairncross (1982), musing on his long experience in the policy arena, concluded, "Economic theory was indispensable for analyzing their problems, but . . . it very rarely allowed one to arrive at policy conclusions with any confidence. Economic theory may elucidate, but certainly does not resolve, controversial issues of economic policy" (p. 3). Good analysis helps decision makers understand what might happen under different courses of action. It does not list five reasons for choosing one approach.

At any time, each of several options will have advantages and disadvantages (Cairncross, 1982, p. 14). Social scientists, especially economists, may feel they can select the optimal approach in their theoretical world (Fraatz, 1983). But, as the Congressional Budget Office economist James Verdier (1984) points out, "Politicians inhabit a world in which they must constantly bargain for outcomes that never wholly satisfy them or anyone else" (p. 423). The economist and longtime presidential advisor Charles Schultze is said to argue that economists must be "advocates for efficiency." But they should not be advocates for a particular approach—only of a way of thinking about alternatives. This is the difference between, respectively, *positive* and *normative* economics.

RULE 6: IDENTIFY WINNERS AND LOSERS

> *Government decision-makers tend to see each alternative as involving an inseparable bundle of consequences. Some involve questions of efficiency; some of equity. And those related to equity are often thought the more important.*
>
> —Christopher Leman and Robert Nelson,
> "Ten Commandments for Policy Economists" (1981)

Decision makers are concerned with how policies affect their constituents, particularly in the immediate future. The political art, according to Thomas Sowell (1996), consists of ostentatious giving and surreptitious taking. Efficiency—usually uppermost in the minds of social scientists—is often a distant second in the minds of decision makers. Social scientists address redistributive consequences vaguely—arguing in favor of policies if those benefiting could, theoretically, compensate those who lose and still come out ahead. Public decision makers cannot afford such abstractions: They face the de facto uncompensated at the next election.

Economists, Steven Rhoads (1978) argues, overlook many aspects of redistributive programs important to decision makers. He illustrates his point with the role of volunteers:

> Over 6,000 people in our community of 100,000 perform volunteer work. One hundred participate in the "Meals on Wheels" Program, donating a few hours a week and driving expenses to take hot meals to elderly people who cannot cook for themselves.
>
> This program is the perfect example of the kind of in-kind redistribution program economists typically attack. The charge would go something like this. "Why have a separate bureaucracy charged with one small thing—delivering hot meals to the elderly? What is so special about a hot meal anyway? Why not give the poor the money we spend on the program to do with as they wish?"
>
> This analysis misses something. The most important thing that the volunteers bring the elderly is not the hot meal, but the human contact and the sense that someone cares. Volunteers can do this more convincingly than bureaucrats.
>
> Perhaps Meals on Wheels is inefficient because this synergistic effect could be more fruitfully attached to some other programmatic vehicle. But the externality concept should in general make economists eager to support policies that seem likely to increase volunteerism. (p. 113)

If social scientists want decision makers to listen to them, they must examine potential winners and losers. Their analyses need make no judgment about whether these outcomes are good or bad. But their skills help them trace through direct and indirect policy impacts.

Social scientists sometimes resist getting involved in distributional issues because they view the world through *optimizing models* that yield a single "best" solution. In the world of political decision makers, however, there are no best solutions, only acceptable ones or ones that are good enough. The Nobel laureate Herbert Simon (1981) coined the word *satisficing* to express this principle. Most political debates arise out of fundamental differences in values, differences that cannot be resolved by empirical analyses. That is why it is so important for analysts to analyze outcomes and not to make recommendations, and the policy analyst's task is to inform the debate over alternatives. The Minnesota representative John Brandl (1985) says, "Politicians see decision-making not as delineating, explication, and choice, but as accommodation, compromise, and, hardest of all, *creation* of a new way of construing an issue so as to satisfy what appear to be antithetical positions of constituencies" (p. 352).

RULE 7: DON'T OVERLOOK UNINTENDED CONSEQUENCES

Most of the serious errors in economic policy committed by governments throughout the ages, and most of the layman's errors in thinking about economic affairs, flow from a failure to consider second order or third order effects of policies.
—Daniel Bell and Irving Kristol, *The Crisis in Economic Theory* (1981)

Many consequences of government action are not intuitively obvious. How will people behave if taxes or regulations are changed? Will local agencies carry out the program as intended? The economic way of thinking allows economists to identify consequences of actions that would be overlooked or misunderstood by people without economic training. Economists are experienced at tracing through the subtle way that incentives work within markets.

For example, economists could have predicted that flood control and insurance programs would encourage building on flood plains. They can often uncover unintended consequences of regulatory policies—hidden costs of trucking regulations, inadvertent harm to consumers during periods of inflation by usury laws, or difficulties of cutting water consumption by regulating its use. And they might have predicted how stimulating mining on public lands through subsidies to mining companies destroyed the land, often irreparably ("How Subsidies Destroy the Land," 1997).

On controversial issues, the discovery of unintended consequences may tilt the balance. These issues are heatedly debated because perceived benefits and costs are closely balanced. New information may be decisive.

Unintended consequences can turn the best-intentioned program into a policy disaster. But application of a little common sense sometimes lets you anticipate these consequences. Decision makers often underestimate the extent to which people will change their behavior to take advantage of opportunities offered by new policies—even if not in the ways envisaged by policymakers. Attempts to tinker with the tax system have often created quite unexpected results. In the late 1970s, New York was losing jobs as companies moved to southern states where, the companies claimed, the tax climate was more favorable. To stem outflow, the New York legislature created a program offering generous tax incentives to businesses that reconsidered their decision to leave and stayed in New York. Stay in New York, program administrators told New York's large businesses, and we will make sure your tax burden is no higher than it would have been had you moved. It sounded like an appropriate response. But the program encouraged all corporations, whether or not they were seriously thinking about relocating out of state, to hire accountants to prepare studies showing how much less taxes were elsewhere. Once the numbers were shown to state officials, tax bills would be slashed. As a result, the cost of abated taxes soared. The absurdity became apparent when a large Fifth Avenue jewelry store was given over $8 million to cover the cost of renovating its already prestigious offices because it threatened to shift its back office operations to New Jersey. Not only was New York losing tens of millions in tax revenues, but it suffered from daily headlines in newspapers about the number of businesses wanting to move out. The legislature eventually shut down the program—gaining it the reputation of being antibusiness.

Federal programs are full of examples of unintended consequences. To target its funds for highway rehabilitation where they were most needed, the Federal Highway Administration released funds to repair only stretches of road that were severely potholed and cracked. Once they understood the rules, state highway administrators delayed or abandoned maintenance programs to accelerate the rate at which their deteriorated roads would become eligible for federal dollars. A program aimed at fixing up highways actually made many roads worse than they would have been without the program.

Or consider the experience of the Environmental Protection Agency (EPA). EPA once ran a program that paid local governments 70% of the costs of building wastewater treatment plants. During the 1970s, this became the nation's largest public works program. Since EPA paid only for construction and not for the operation of the plants, local governments tried to make the facilities as automated as possible—employing all kinds of automatic devices and untried, and often unsuccessful, technologies that vastly inflated construction costs. EPA made matters worse by offering special incentives to local governments whose treatment facilities embodied "new technologies." Not only were these high-tech plants expensive but most proved so unreliable they had to be rebuilt. When federal subsidies were cut and responsibility for financing wastewater investments was returned to state and local governments, the projections of investment levels needed to comply with the Clean Water Act plummeted: Faced with paying for projects themselves, local governments quickly found cheaper ways to meet targets.

In these examples, unintended consequences are caused by the perverse incentive structure built into program operation. The moral is simple: Businesses and public administrators will do whatever is in their power to take advantage of policies and programs paid for by someone else. Unintended, and undesirable, consequences also occur because decision makers try to regulate management of the bureaucracy. Instead of setting public program goals, procedures under which programs operate, decision makers try to set strict procedures—procedures intended to eliminate waste, fraud, and abuse. The result may cut fraud and abuse, but often at a cost of enormous waste. Consider these stories described by Vice President Al Gore (1993) in *The Report of the National Performance Review:*

> The district managers of Oregon's million-acre Ochoco National Forest have 53 separate budgets—one for fence maintenance, one for fence construction, one for brush burning—divided into 557 management codes and 1,769 accounting lines. To transfer money between accounts, they need approval from headquarters. They estimate the task of tracking spending in each account consumes at least 30 days of their time every year, days they could spend doing their real jobs. It also sends a message: You are not trusted with even the simplest responsibilities.
>
> The U.S. Merit Systems Protection Board reports there are now 850 pages of federal personnel law—augmented by 1,300 pages of Office of Personnel Management regulations on how to implement those laws and another 10,000 pages of guidelines from the Federal Personnel Manual. . . . The full stack of personnel laws, regulations, directives, case law, and department guidance that the Department of Agriculture uses weighs 1,088 pounds. (p. 72)

Explaining how indirect consequences arise is not easy. It often requires a chain of reasoning running counter to our intuitive understanding of how things work. And indirect consequences are often much less visible than more direct consequences—even though, in aggregate effect, they may far exceed the direct and visible consequences. When a steel plant closes, for example, many people will blame cheap imported steel and call for limits on how much foreign steel is allowed across our borders. The policy analyst will struggle to explain the potential consequences of trade restrictions. Indirect benefits from free trade (lower consumer prices, new products, and more jobs in export industries) are diffused throughout the economy whereas the closed steel plant stands as visible evidence of the costs. People believe that the nation is harmed by trade. Or, as economists have long pointed out, although employers *nominally* pay payroll taxes—such as unemployment insurance and a portion of worker's compensation—the real burden is born by wage earners. Employers balance the value of what employees contribute against the total cost of hiring them—higher fringe benefits mean lower wages. Politicians will always define an "equitable" tax as one in which the burden is shared by employers and employees. Economists have also shown that severance taxes are not paid by the out-of-state power companies buying the oil or coal (because international prices are unaffected by state and local taxes). Severance taxes, in reality, are paid by those who own the mineral rights and who are paid a lower royalty by mining companies because of the severance taxes they must pay.

These arguments failed to persuade many decision makers. Whenever decision makers are forced to choose between instinct and the logical products of technical analyses (however scholarly) instinct generally wins. After all, others share our instincts, so we explain our instinctive decisions more easily than our logical ones. When policy analysts must challenge conventional wisdom or intuition, they should choose their fights carefully and inspect the terrain of battle in advance.

Policy analysts should view their task as preparing the information needed to make a decision. Their task is not assembling facts to justify a single approach, however unambiguous conclusions appear from their analysis. Trusted policy analysts will be asked for their opinion, but that opinion should not govern the message. The message experts must convey to the decision maker will carry far less than the experts know about the topic but more than the experts are accustomed to sharing.

SUMMARY

Policy analysts, having completed their analysis, must communicate it effectively to decision makers, just as physicians must communicate their work to patients, relatives, and others—nurses, pharmacists, allied health professionals, social workers, and so on. Policy analysts, when communicating analysis, become involved in politics and advocacy at their own risk: Policy analysts must focus only on policy. Decision makers prefer reading analysis that is simple, explains the reasoning behind alternatives and interpretations, reveals winners and losers, and identifies long-term, unintended consequences. Even though policy analysts may have spent untold hours reviewing studies, methods, information, and data, decision makers are only interested in the pared-down results of this work.

8

Deciding How to Say It

> *Galileo's* Dialogo *succeeded not because it was a*
> *Copernican tract (there were others) or because it contained*
> *much new evidence (it did not) but because it was a masterpiece*
> *of Italian prose. Poincaré's French and Einstein's German*
> *were no trivial elements in their influence. And of course the*
> *hypnotic influence that Keynes has exercised over modern*
> *economics is attributable in part to his graceful style.*
> —Donald McCloskey, "Economical Writing" (1985a, p. 189)

Once we've decided what we want decision makers to know, we have to figure out how to communicate it. We must communicate clearly—not just clear enough to be understood, but clear enough so that we cannot be misunderstood. And we must communicate in a way that compels the decision maker's attention (Yanow, 1996). Policy—or medical—writing does not have to be awful (Halpert, 1990; Zinsser, 1994).

The object of writing is to be read. Bad writing—whatever the merits of its content—will not be read. To communicate with decision makers, we must compete for every minute of their attention in the noisy market for ideas (see, especially, Maraniss, 1996). At any minute, the reader can get up and leave. And if the reader leaves, the writer has no one but himself or herself to blame. Good writing saves readers' time, gives them information they need to know, and inspires confidence in underlying arguments. Thomas Jefferson is said to have said, "The most valuable of all talents is that of never using two words when one will do."

Good policy analysis must be brief, persuasive, and readable—like a good Op-Ed article in a newspaper, telling a clear, logical, and compelling story (see also, McCloskey, 1990). It illustrates major points with a few telling facts. It is topical; avoids jargon, long words, and equations; and attacks neither people with differing views nor those views. Decision makers must explain their actions to constituents and to the public. Good analysis must provide those explanations. Writing clearly means abandoning jargon. Congressman Lee Hamilton (1992), the once-powerful vice chairperson of the Joint Economic Committee of Congress recently wrote, "The most important quality for economists to have when they are testifying or advising policy-makers is the ability to express their ideas on important policy issues clearly and simply, without jargon" (p. 61; Andreski, 1972).

If we cannot write clearly, we cannot think clearly. The underground grammarian Richard Mitchell (1979) crusaded among academics for greater attention to the communication arts:

> Language is, essentially, speech. Writing is a special case of language. Discursive prose is a special case of writing. . . . It is no coincidence that the Greeks who first devised discursive prose also constructed formal logic. Thinking is coherent discourse, and the logic and the prose require one another. The mind is a rudderless wanderer blown here or there by any puff of breeze. . . . The very rare genius can keep his mind on course for a while, perhaps as long as a whole minute, but most of us are always at the mercy of every random suggestion of environment. . . . If we want to pursue extended logical thought, thought that can discover relationships and consequences and devise its own alternatives, we need a discipline imposed from outside the mind. Writing is that discipline. It seems drastic, but we have to suspect that continuous thought is impossible for those who cannot construct coherent, continuous prose. "Writing," Bacon said, "maketh an exact man." (pp. 39-40)

To write more effectively, learn to rewrite (Zinsser, 1994). The goal of rewriting is to cut words, sentences, even paragraphs, without sacrificing argument or information. This art is not a free lunch from the gods. Like mathematics or bicycle riding, rewriting must be learned. And it is best learned by writing. The fastest way to learn is by applying simple rules to the task of writing and rewriting. The economist John Kenneth Galbraith (1978), a fine stylist, admits that "there are days when the result is so bad that no fewer than five revisions are required. In contrast, when the day goes well, only four revisions are needed" (p. 103).

This chapter lays out simple and concise rules for writing and rewriting. With practice, you will think more logically and communicate more effectively. Obeying the rules laid out in the following pages does not destroy style. By being brief and clear, your own style will better emerge—as a garden develops when weeds are removed. Style is the end, not the beginning, of good writing. The philosopher Alfred North Whitehead said,

Style, in its finest sense, is the last acquirement of the educated mind: it is also the most useful. It pervades the whole being. The administrator with a sense of style hates waste; the engineer with a sense of style economizes his material; the artisan with a sense of style prefers good work. Style is the ultimate morality of the mind.

RULE 1: WRITE TO THINK

None of us really knows what we mean until we see it in words (Yanow, 1996). Setting out arguments on paper forces us to ask new questions and explore new logical links. "Writing," says the planning professor Martin Krieger (1988), "leads to a making-sense of the world you did not know you possessed" (p. 56). The Austrian critic Karl Kraus believed that speech was the mother, not the handmaid, of thought. And Zinsser (1994) opines, "Writing is how we think our way into a subject and make it our own. Writing enables us to find out what we know—and what we don't know—about whatever we're trying to learn" (p. 24).

Most formal academic training, however, focuses on the mastery of technical skills, ignoring writing and communication. Many academic journals give the strong impression that clear communication is of lower priority. Writing up results is an afterthought to the conduct of scientific investigation. Yet, our reputation and our ideas live only through our communication—in speech, sometimes, but most often in writing.

Many of us—particularly if we've written a lot—think we're better writers than we actually are (see, e.g., Sypher & Zorn, 1986). Our readers may not agree. We have the advantage over readers: We know what we meant when we chose our words. Or we may delude ourselves into believing we know what we meant. Readers, lacking this thoughtful context, cannot understand us. Reader and writer travel in opposite directions, the former advancing from language to thought, the latter from thought to language. The reader must reconstitute the writer's thoughts from clues provided by the few written words and phrases. Unless those words are chosen carefully and organized logically, reconstitution is impossible—even by the most diligent reader.

RULE 2: DON'T FEAR FIRST DRAFTS

Policy analysis is an unpredictable world of deadlines. Policy analysts rarely have time to wait until they feel like writing. Circumstances may conspire to create writer's block. Do not even try to make your first draft a polished document. Write down all the facts and arguments. Leave blanks and put down half-formed ideas. "Get the thinking straight," advises David Osborne, author of *Reinventing Government* (Osborne & Gaebler, 1992),

> before worrying about the composition. I was taught to make outlines. I have since taught others to make detailed outlines before writing, and to a person, they have found the advice useful. A detailed outline allows you to think through the writing before you have to worry about style. Thinking through the arguments, their order, the evidence you want to marshal, etc., is a difficult but essential task. Choosing the right words is another difficult but essential task. Separating the two makes a writer's job far, far easier. I am convinced that much of the paralysis people experience in front of a blank page (or screen) is a symptom of trying to do two things at once: figure out what comes next, and figure out how to say it. (p. 10)

Once you've completed a first draft, then rewrite, rewrite, and rewrite, clarifying main arguments, building transitions, and eliminating unnecessary material. Then, and only then, circulate the draft for comment. Always spare others the burden of reviewing first drafts, or even second drafts, however tight the deadline. Vladimir Nabokov believed, "Only ambitious nonentities and hearty mediocrities exhibit their rough drafts." The purpose of circulating a draft is to attract comment on ideas, logic, or style. First drafts accurately express neither the author's ideas nor his or her style. And when you get comments, pay attention to them. If a reader claims a passage is unclear, rewrite it; don't accuse the reader of careless reading. "I learned never to defend anything I had written against the accusation that it is not clear enough," advised the philosopher of science, Karl Popper. "If a conscientious reader finds a passage unclear it has to be rewritten. . . . I write, as it were with someone constantly looking over my shoulder and constantly pointing out passages which are not clear" (quoted in McCloskey, 1985a, p. 191).

Circulating first drafts among politicians is dangerous. Carelessly worded arguments will be torn out of context and no amount of rewriting can overcome the first misunderstanding. It is axiomatic of policy making that the first distributed draft is the only one that matters. Norman Mailer observed, "Once a newspaper touches a story, the facts are lost forever, even to the protagonists."

Do not wait for inspiration. The writer Frank Yerby actually advises, "I quit writing if I feel inspired, because I know I'm going to have to throw it away. Writing is like building a wall brick by brick. Only an amateur believes in inspiration."

Do not fear of criticism. Sometimes writer's block stems from the fear of criticism. In *The Inner Game of Writing*, Martin Krieger (1988) recommends creating a "non-judgmental arena in which the analyst writes what might be called a transitional draft—playing, yet committed to the real product" (p. 56). Too often policy analysts equate criticism of their work with attacks on their person. Focus on the former, eschew the latter.

Do not be captive of preconceived ideas—writing a first draft should produce surprising new insights and logical links. The act of putting down thoughts and making arguments for the first time should spur the imagination.

When you get stuck, try these 10 ways to start your first draft:

1. *Reread your "purpose statement" and the outline.* Use each sentence from the outline as the point of departure for draft sections—in whatever order is most comfortable.

2. *Create cooker sheets.* Write subject words, thoughts, outline entries, and so on at the top of a blank sheet. Divide the sheet horizontally into thirds. Label the top third, *First Thoughts;* the second, *Queries;* and the third, *New Directions.*

3. *Seize the moment.* When you start developing new thoughts on a topic, don't let anyone or anything interrupt. Disconnect your telephone, lock your office door, or dim the lights if you have to.

4. *Write the frosting first.* Don't get stuck on writing in the order that the paper will be read. Start with the parts that you are most interested in. Word processing allows authors to move textual material around at will. Produce the bricks, then construct the house.

5. *Get cranky.* Convert your panic into anger over some aspect of the topic about which you feel strongly. But discard any evidence of your nastiness. Having vented, you will be ready to work.

6. *Free-associate.* Give yourself a time limit—5 to 15 minutes—during which you must keep the cursor moving across the screen, writing about anything.

7. *Talk instead of writing.* Many of us want our writing to be formal and choke in front of a blank sheet of paper or computer screen. Yet, we can speak freely on our topic. Imagine you are explaining the topic to an interested friend, and talk. Transcribe and edit your thoughts.

8. *Leave signposts.* It's natural to run out of steam before finishing—but, before you quit, leave signposts for the next writing session. These may be ideas, key words, topics, or headings—anything that transfers energy from this session to the next.

9. *Reread past output before moving on.* This reminds you of where you were going and how you were getting there.

10. *Change the format.* When Tom Wolfe was blocked on an article about customized cars, he wrote a memo to his editor on the subject that the editor published as the article. New ideas can be released by switching format, even if it means telling a fairy story ("Once upon a time there were three theories . . . "), writing a Dick and Jane book ("See the garbage pile up"), or composing a cable ("Extension of training program advised. Increased funding subject to two conditions . . . ") or a letter to a friend ("I have to write a report and I need your help").
11. *Change tools.* Try switching from the computer to a legal pad.

RULE 3: SHOW, DON'T TELL

Academics are used to telling things to their students. Students, for their part, are used to writing down what they are told. Telling works well as a pedagogical approach, but it is not a good way of communicating with decision makers. Experts must forget classroom techniques when they prepare to advise decision makers. Advisors must show their readers or listeners what the problem is, how the problem could be tackled, and the advantages and disadvantages of each approach. A policy paper that is written in the tone "Present housing policy is a disaster and the only way to fix it is to. . . " will attract few readers and make fewer converts. Many intended readers likely played an important part in formulating and administering present housing policy. If, instead, the paper describes symptoms of housing problems; provides a calm, convincing diagnosis of what causes the problems; and lays out the pros and cons, it will hold the readers' attention and may persuade them of underlying arguments.

To hold the audience, writers must maintain a consistent and direct tone. But academic training encourages us to keep a podium between ourselves and our audience, eliminating personal contact between writer and reader. The writer hides behind arcane language and impersonal passives—rituals of professional communication (McCloskey, 1985b). Readers experience no feel for the person whose judgment they are trying to assess.

Reestablish contact with the reader by following these steps:

Step 1. Visualize the audience. Aim writing directly at people you want to inform. We are easily tempted to write for as large an audience as possible—at the very least, for the annual meeting of our branch of the social sciences; at the most, for all of posterity. But the bigger the audience, the greater the risk of losing intimacy and immediacy. Writing is like making a speech—most effective when delivered to the audience, not over its head at the cameras. If you write about a new way to manage local schools, for example, aim your paper at education administrators first, and parents and teachers second. Focus. Do not shift in mid-paper to embrace the entire American people, all schoolchildren, or members of Congress. Since many other people are interested in education, they may "eavesdrop" if the message to administrators is interesting and clear. But write for eavesdroppers, and the primary audience will lose interest. And so will the eavesdroppers.

To avoid the trap of writing for fellow social scientists, fix your mind on someone you know who is interested in the issue and may be in a position similar to the intended audience. Then write for that person. Do not be afraid to write in the first person. "Writing is, after all," says William Zinsser (1994), "a personal transaction between two people" (p. 22). You will find yourself more relaxed and less likely to resort to cumbersome, impersonal phrases if "you" write as an individual, rather than hiding behind a pompous "you," an arid "one," or an anonymous passive.

Step 2. Figure out who you are—at least for as long as you are writing the paper. William Zinsser (1994) offers a checklist to work through before beginning to write:

1. In what capacity am I going to address the reader?
2. What style? Impersonal reportorial? Personal but formal? Personal but casual?
3. What attitude am I going to take toward the material? Involved? Detached? Judgmental? Ironic? Amused?

Once you've answered each of these questions, do not switch in mid-course.

Adopt a distant academic tone and decision makers will feel you are talking down to them. Deviate from normal speech and you reveal more than you wanted about how you view yourself and your professional role. Remember that decision makers want to judge the expert as a person, not as a technician. "Desire for status is one reason academic men slip so readily into unintelligibility," says the sociologist C. Wright Mills (1961). "To overcome the academic prose you first have to overcome the academic pose" (p. 218). To dispense with the podium, he recommends asking:

1. How difficult and complex after all is the subject? I do not want to demonstrate technical virtuosity, but to appeal to the reader's common sense.
2. When I write, what status am I claiming for myself? The good analyst is a conduit of useful information, not the final authority.

Step 3. Avoid hysteria. Shedding academic tone is no reason to become overwrought. If you feel strongly about an issue, you may feel tempted to let passion overcome clarity. The 1980s becomes a "decade of greed." Ranchers become "desecrators of the western landscape." The homeless become "victims of the crisis in housing affordability." Writers who succumb to stylistic pyrotechnics lose their objectivity, and then, since decision makers wanted analysis not advocacy, analysts lose their readers.

It's easy to detect hysteria: Adjectives and adverbs give you away. "Very," "absolutely," "vital," "disastrous," "critical," and their synonyms convey a tone the reader is unlikely to share. Superlatives and extremes ("the worst aspect . . . ," "the only way . . . ," "it is imperative that . . . ") crowd out logical argument. Moral imperatives—"should," "must," and "ought"—replace reasoning.

Let the decision makers judge what is important. Remember, you are showing them, not telling them. Don't demand that they adopt your position. Strunk and White (1979) note wryly, "To air one's views gratuitously . . . is to imply that the demand for them is brisk" (p. 80). McCloskey (1985a) adds, "and to air them intemperately reduces whatever demand there is" (p. 204). Keep the tone cool and do not whine. The world is quickly bored by the recital of misfortunes and willingly avoids the sight of distress. If others don't listen to you, don't blame them. Figure out how to communicate more effectively.

Step 4: Sympathize with opposing views. It's tempting to gloat on paper if we find flaws in the arguments of opponents; it is the stuff of tenure to accuse opponents of ignorance or worse. But decision makers you wish to persuade may hold similar views and will be alienated by a verbal victory dance. As a rule, never begin writing—especially on controversial issues—until you understand and sympathize with different points of view. It is often useful to start by discussing opposing views, sympathizing with why a reasonable person might hold them. In this way, you will give readers a much better chance of understanding the flaw—if there is a flaw—in their reasoning. The decision maker will recognize that you are not someone who is theologically opposed to his or her views: After all, reasonable people can disagree over theology. They will recognize that you struggled with the same ideas and that because you uncovered new information or a new way of looking at the issue you came to a different conclusion. Doctrinal clashes are not crises, but opportunities. Always present opposing views as plausible ways of looking at issues; never treat those who disagree as heathens ripe for conversion.

Decision makers need to anticipate what opponents will say. Good policy analysis explains major arguments against different approaches and discusses how to deal with them. To counter the argument that adjacent states have adopted a policy, the analyst might identify differences in institutions or economic circumstances or unfavorable evaluations.

Step 5. Don't share the hardships of collecting and analyzing data. You are not trying to justify how you spent a research grant or why you should be given another one. Resist the temptation to show decision makers how much you know. Keep in mind the image of the rushed, perhaps harried, reader. Never assume decision makers will struggle through your prose because it is relevant or, worse, because you wrote it. They won't. At best, they will commission another analyst to summarize your work, often to your detriment.

Picture yourself sitting next to the reader, with no podium between you, explaining the issue clearly and quickly.

Step 6. Do not be afraid to state your own views. Academics often believe in theory, at least—they should say no more than evidence supports. That is why so many academic articles end with conclusions describing the implications of the reported research in very narrow terms—customarily adding a plea for further research. Yet, decision makers must decide what to do without benefit of further research: Policy making requires judgment, and decision makers often get understandably irritated by experts who resist sharing their own judgments. The expert's opinion about likely consequences of different policies is valuable information. It should not be withheld.

The Economist, one of the few magazines willing to let its writers state their views, offers the following advice for anyone trying to inform economic policy decisions:

> Economists must sometimes be as sad as nuclear scientists at the damage that an idea can do. Time and again they produce a new theory and then, the interesting part over with, make some tentative suggestions for policy—only to find that when the idea is taken up, it all goes wrong. . . . The trouble seems to be that governments use only bits of the new theory, or all of it plus some out-dated bits of another one, or they only pretend to use it while actually doing what they thought of in the first place.
>
> If economists are to be understood let them use plainer words. Which prompts two other thoughts for making ideas more hijack-proof. First address those words less to politicians and more to everyone else. Politicians care about what voters think, especially voters in blocks. Talking to

politicians about economics is therefore a waste of time. The only way to make governments behave as if they were economically literate is to confront them with electorates that are.

Second, and to that end, do not stress the mainly macroeconomic issues (such as monetary and fiscal policy) where technical disagreements are rife and the scope for making most economies better off is anyway slim. Try instead to build a popular consensus on the microeconomic issues (above all, trade) where economists are largely in agreement, and where the gains to be had from sensible policies are truly immense. That sort of economics would be more useful—and, with luck, a bit less dangerous. ("Economic Policy Advice," 1985, pp. 10-11)

Step 7. Write for the ear, not the eye. Readers "hear" what they read because they read with their lips—even if those lips don't move. Bad writing sounds bad read aloud. Therefore, writers must be part poet— concerned with how writing sounds as well as its grammatical correctness. Most turgid prose clogging academic journals is grammatically correct. "In conversation," says the novelist Erica Jong, "you can use timing, a look, inflection, pauses. But on the page all you have is commas, dashes, the number of syllables in a word. When I write I read everything out loud to get the right rhythm."

Decision makers know how arguments sound. They want to use key sentences or phrases from experts in speeches to persuade colleagues and constituents or clarify issue stances. Prose that sounds good is simple, not full of purple passages. Some of the most memorable political lines express ideas with such simplicity and clarity that we cannot forget them ("Ask not what your country can do for you . . . ").

RULE 4: BE BRIEF AND CLEAR

Good policy analysis helps decision makers understand issues by being brief and clear and telling a compelling story. Politicians are most easily engaged in something that is the length of the typical article appearing on the page of a newspaper opposite the editorials—about 600-800 words. Their staff may need technical background to support the central argument if they intend to develop legislation or write regulations. But the core argument must be brief. Wherever possible, place technical material in appendices so it doesn't clutter the basic argument.

These steps can help you write less and with greater clarity:

Step 1. Select the core story and stick to it. Decision makers should gain one original insight from your paper, for example, changing the tax code will reduce business failures, an agriculture support policy costs consumers more than it helps farmers, or liberalization of trade policy will not harm a local industry. There are always many other interesting things to be said about any issue. But busy readers remember few arguments, especially if they depend on complex reasoning. The central argument should be made in several different ways (by anecdote in the opening paragraph, with supporting data in the central paragraphs, and by corollary in the closing paragraph, for example).

Decision makers suffer from unmanageable information overload; government agencies, trade associations, lobbyists, newspapers, magazines, think tanks, universities, people at cocktail parties, and streams of petitioners deluge them with data. According to one survey, the average congressional representative works an 11-hour day but spends only 11 minutes reading (Verdier, 1984; see also, Manzullo, 1996; Maraniss, 1996). That's not enough time to digest a long report—or to make sense of a confusing short one. Because decision makers are rushed and concerned with specific issues, they must know from the first few sentences why they should read on. Therefore, the first paragraph must tell readers who the paper is intended for and what issues it covers. Information is not necessarily a good thing. The economist Kenneth Boulding (1966b) argued, "Knowledge is always gained by the orderly loss of information, that is, by condensing and abstracting the great buzzing confusion that comes from the world around us into a form that we can appreciate and comprehend" (p. 26).

Step 2. Use headings and table titles to advance your argument. Headings and even table captions should be informative, preferably declarative sentences. Titling a section "State Economic Performance: 1980-1990" is empty. Try "During the 1980s, State Employment Doubled." This tells readers what they need most to remember. A table headed "Income Growth by Sector" is deadly. "Income Grew in All Industries Except Manufacturing" leaves the reader with the message.

Step 3. Don't whiplash the reader. Stick to the story. The writer's task is to give the reader a small-scale but useful map of large terrain. A description of the seven ways that a tax increase could influence economic development with the conclusion that there is no evidence of any effects at all will anger rather than inform the reader. Lead with the conclusion and focus the writing on amplifying that central point. You may want to point out why people have been mistaken in their belief that taxes determine local development. But make the point directly. Your job is to give the reader compelling reasons for agreeing with and believing in your argument. Avoid hosting a surprise party at the end.

RULE 5: BUILD THE STORY WITH PARAGRAPHS

All policy papers follow more or less the same overall structure:

1. An attention-grabbing lead
2. A brief summary of the thesis
3. Structural clues to the paper
4. Major point 1, major point 2, major point 3, etc.
5. Conclusion

Paragraphs are a writer's basic building blocks, and paragraph breaks will reflect the paper's outline. The usual paragraph should be long enough to complete a thought, short enough to give the reader some visible hope of relief, and middling enough not to look odd alongside its fellows. Do not be afraid to use single sentence—or, if you are really daring, single word, paragraphs. But use them sparingly—only to draw attention to an argument or a change of direction.

Step 1. Craft an engaging opening. The most important paragraph is the first one. It must give the reader a compelling reason for reading on. It is your only chance to get someone to read what you have written. It must compete for the reader's scarce time with thousands of other articles, papers, books, TV, and the telephone. Capture the reader with freshness, paradox, or humor.

> Forget sex, lies and audiotapes: to a British observer, the extraordinary revelation in the coverage of the Bill Clinton affair was the report that the White House employed 250 interns. With so many competitors for the president's ear, no wonder some of them are alleged to focus on other parts of his anatomy. ("Size Isn't Everything," 1998, p. 60)

Op-Ed articles are a rich source of techniques for grabbing readers. Analyze why you felt compelled to read a piece in your morning paper. No opening numbs readers faster than the traditional, "The purpose of this paper is to analyze the problem of health care for the uninsured." Show, don't tell readers, why the issue is important. Would it work better to begin: "This year, local hospitals will treat 3,000 people who have no health insurance. This will cost other patients an extra $235 for each day in hospital. What are the cheaper and fairer ways of caring for indigent people?" Beginning your piece with dire threats of impending crisis unless action is taken may lose you readers. Depict problems as opportunities to improve matters, not as the end of civilization.

Step 2. End briefly and appropriately. The second most important paragraph is the last. It's your final attempt to convey your message. The closing should not drag. Omit such padding as "in conclusion," or "the final point that must be made is that . . . " The closing should never raise new points.

Step 3. Wire paragraphs in series, not in parallel. Each paragraph should advance the plot a step—neither more nor less. Each paragraph should amplify and build on the one that precedes it. Make sure that the closing of one paragraph or the opening of the next include logical transitions so that the passage from one to the next is smooth. Smooth transitions are achieved through words or phrases that look backward, tying the paragraph to what has come before. If there is an abrupt change in direction between paragraphs, warn the reader—begin the new paragraph with a mood changing word: "But," "Yet," "Despite . . . " If you can change the order of your paragraphs and not lose the thread of your story, you are not telling a story. But don't overdo linkages, forward or backward. Assume that readers are intelligent and attentive and able to understand connections you make.

Step 4. Be aware of the rhythms within paragraphs. If all sentences are the same length, they become boring. Complex arguments usually require long sentences. Emphatic conclusions need short ones. Each sentence in the paragraph should amplify the central theme of the paragraph. A paragraph's topic should be summarized in a single sentence—the first sentence if possible. Engaging the reader begins with a question or even a sentence fragment or word. But do not use this technique too often. A quick scan of opening sentences of paragraphs should give the reader a summary of major points and logic of your arguments. For busy decision makers, topic sentences may be all they care to read. Make paragraphs hang together internally by repeating words and creating links. These might be simply a word or phrase: "Therefore," "Again," or "For the same reason"). But transition can also be achieved through repetition. Repeat, and paragraphs hang together.

RULE 6: WRITE CLEAR SENTENCES

Sentences should be specific, definite, concrete. Few are—at least at first attempt. As we struggle to put down our thoughts, we burden sentences with too many ideas. We cram in subordinate clauses and phrases with asides, auxiliary thoughts, and odd bits of information seemingly important. We start a sentence going one way but backtrack to fill in missing material. That's fine for a first draft. As long as it is rewritten.

But rewriting is difficult. We swell with parental pride in our own images or phrases, blinding us to their flaws. Often, we are too lazy to rewrite, so we convince ourselves that our work is fine. Other times, we may hope that the decision makers will not notice our transgressions or, if they do notice, will be forgiving. Here are some steps to guide the task of rewriting:

Step 1: Ask yourself "so what" as you reread each sentence. Force each sentence to work. Empty sentences clutter most academic prose: "There are many ways in which taxes influence economic development," or "Demographic forces play an important role in the housing market." Describe those "influences" and "roles"—don't announce them first. Replace empty sentences with nutritionally complete sentences containing hard, useful facts or arguments. Sentences such as "Changes in the price of water influence household behavior" have no place in policy analysis because they do not inform the reader of the nature of the change. On the other hand, the sentence "Households cut water use by 50% if prices are doubled" conveys directly useful information.

When you ask "so what?" about your sentence, you should provide only one answer. Each sentence should make one point, no more, no less. Cramming two points into a single sentence diminishes the importance of both.

Step 2. Make sentences vivid and concrete. Even if the sentence has substance, it may be too general for the reader. Sentences such as "Training programs that work best provide people with the skills needed in the marketplace," or "Environmental regulations should take account of the costs of abatement" require the reader to work, converting them into concrete proposals. How do you know when a training program provides appropriate skills? A short list of skills in demand would have made the sentence more vivid. Which programs provide those skills? It helps to name a few successful programs—especially if the paper discusses them elsewhere. How should abatement costs be measured?

Listing some of costs would help. Who should measure the costs? Name the agency. Many readers will not bother with the extra work you ask them to perform. Worse yet, readers may countenance the wrong meaning when left on their own. The hard work of understanding details of carrying out policies should be undertaken by the analyst, not the decision maker.

Academics tend to be too general because the social sciences deal in general relationships among concepts, not in specific relationships among real organizations and people. But most people understand the world in concrete terms. Instead of using an abstract phrase such as "program costs," list costs you mean to include: "rents, payrolls, and utility bills." Make specific agencies or offices the subject of sentences instead of the abstract "government" or "the public sector." Describe how "the corporate income tax" or "property taxes," not "taxes" in general, influence business decisions.

Step 3. Build sentences around action verbs. Use verbs to express actions rather than to state conditions. Sentences built around the verb to be or based on weak verbs such as provide, require, do, or make don't create strong images. The strongest sentences are those in which the subject does something. Each sentence should state who's doing what in the subject, what that who is doing in the verb, and to whom it is done in the object.

Step 4. Choose sentence length deliberately. The average sentence should not be long. If a sentence contains more than 20-25 words, it should have a good reason for it. Information is best assimilated in digestible bites. If you need to impart a lot of complex information on a single topic, tabulate or use bullets or some other visual device that helps the reader recognize five or six parallel points.

Is it ever appropriate to have single word sentences? Yes. But not too often or the reader may feel treated as a simpleton. Some software editing programs provide average sentence word counts. Use them as a way of becoming aware of how long your sentences are. Then you can vary length deliberately, as a matter of style.

When you use lists, make sure that each piece of information is parallel. Five functions of a proposed law should not switch from "1) to require companies to register hazardous waste" to " 5) encouraging the development of waste disposal technologies." Do not begin one with an infinitive, another with an action verb, and another with an abstract noun.

Step 5. Vary sentences by putting different emphasis and weight into subject, verb, and object. Another aspect of a sentence's structure you can use consciously to improve style is where you place its emphasis. How much attention the reader pays to a word depends on where it falls in the sentence. The place of greatest emphasis is at the end. The beginning is the next most important place. Information placed in the middle of a sentence will be paid the least attention.

Consider three versions of the same sentence:

1. This year, the number of homeless people seeking public shelter more than doubled.
2. The number of homeless people seeking public shelter more than doubled this year.
3. This year, double the number of homeless people sought public shelter.

Although each sentence contains more or less the same number of words, different placing leads to different emphasis. Whereas the first sentence emphasizes the increase in the number of homeless people (it doubled), the last sentence emphasizes changes in what the homeless people did (they sought public shelter).

Step 6. Use punctuation to make sentences as clear as possible. Punctuation is a tool you can use to make sentences more readable. It is not an arcane set of rules invented by grammarians to make life difficult for writers. Punctuation lets you establish the rhythm your readers hear as they read what you've written. Without punctuation, sentences acquire a flat, rapid-fire feel. String together several unpunctuated sentences, and your prose becomes repetitive. The reader's attention wanders.

But don't overpunctuate. Rearrange sentences to reduce the number of commas, dashes, or semicolons by putting clauses at the beginning or end of the sentence. When you interrupt the flow, do it for emphasis. Punctuation marks, like words, are not "free goods": They take the reader's time.

Step 7. Keep related words together. Don't separate the subject from the principle verb with phrases or clauses. For example, the sentence, "President Clinton opposed the Republican welfare reform bill after assessing its impact on public opinion," is better structurally than, "President Clinton, after assessing its impact on public opinion, opposed the Republican welfare reform bill." Avoid breaking the sentence flow with parenthetical remarks. "The Republican welfare reform bill (the last of three major attempts to pass strong legislation) passed with bipartisan support" as a sentence contains distracting parenthetical information. Put such remarks at the end of the sentence if they are important, at the beginning if they are not.

RULE 7: OMIT NEEDLESS WORDS

Since we have so little time to engage the reader and convey our message, we should do so with as few words as possible. Strike out repetitive sentences, restructure and combine sentences, and find single words to do the work of several. "Clutter is the disease of American writing," writes William Zinsser (1994). "We are a society strangling in unnecessary words, circular constructions, pompous frills and meaningless jargon. . . . The secret of good writing is to strip every sentence to its cleanest components" (p. 7)

When writing first drafts, we often measure progress by how much we wrote. When rewriting, measure progress by how much you cut out. The writing principle with the fewest exceptions is: Any way to cut words without losing clarity is an improvement—less is always more. Each word on the page takes additional time and effort to interpret.

Step 1. Use one word to mean one thing. Avoid "elegant variation"— using different words to refer to the same subject (people should not change from "consumers" in one sentence to "householders" in the next to "individuals" later). Remember that terms favored by economists— such as "cost," "value," "benefit"—have different meanings to non-economists. Once defined, repeat them; don't use synonyms.

Step 2. Avoid unnecessary abstraction. A string of nouns held together with prepositions and relying on the passive voice is a common fault with social scientific writing. By trying to remain impersonal and detached, writers sound flabby and obscure. Most nominalizations— nouns created from verbs that usually end in "-ion"—should be rewritten as action verbs "Our intention is to . . . " should become "we intend . . . " Never talk of decisions: Always decide. But nominalizations can be powerful at the end of a sentence ("That is not my intention" is stronger than "I do not intend to").

Step 3. Do not digress. Include no asides about mistakes in previous research (". . . , which differs from the results in Z, who failed to . . . "), parenthetical technical definitions ("what has frequently been called the communications revolution"), or esoteric references to the finer "isms" of our disciplines ("an effect first identified in a seminal paper by . . . ").

Step 4. Avoid passive verbs (and passive people). Rearrange sentences to reduce the number of words and eliminate passives and weak words such "is" and "are." Passives obscure who is performing the action, making policy recommendations unclear. If "a task force is to be convened" we don't know who will be responsible. Without the specific injunction, "The Secretary of Commerce should convene a task force," no one else is likely to volunteer.

There are seven cases when passives may be preferred (Good, 1989, p. 120):

1. When the identity of the actor is the punch of the sentence, e.g., *The tapes were hidden by the President of the United States.*
2. When the identity of the actor is irrelevant, e.g., *The policy was established in 1988.*
3. When the identity of the actor is unknown, e.g., *The tapes were mysteriously destroyed.*
4. When you want to hide the identity of the actor, e.g., *I regret to inform you that the file has been misplaced.*
5. When you want to avoid sexist writing, e.g., *An application for employment must be filed with the personnel office.*
6. When the passive sounds better, e.g., *Consumers are sometimes exploited by disreputable sellers.*
7. When the recipient of the action is the subject of the rest of the paragraph, e.g., *Smith has lasted in the Department for more than a year. Nevertheless he will probably be asked to resign.*

But these cases are exceptions, too rare to justify habitual passives. Each time a passive is used, it should be justified by reference to these rules.

Step 5. Don't state or restate the obvious. Readers can make straightforward causal inferences for themselves—and they are likely to feel insulted if the writer overlooks their skills. Never, ever, begin a sentence with the clause "It is important to note that . . . " If it's not important to note something, presumably we would not write it down. Everything we write is important. Sentences should be so constructed that the reader learns what is important.

Step 6. Don't clot prose with traffic directions. Sentences should be so organized that prior announcements are unnecessary. Avoid "it is interesting to note that" "not only . . . but also," "in addition," "on one hand . . . on the other"). If something is worth adding, add it; don't announce that you're going to add it first. If it's not worth adding, don't. Forget the rule, "Say what you're going to say, say it, and say what you've said." Instead, tell a story. Many papers wade through oceans of data, making the text the verbal equivalent of tables. Text should follow the contours of the data, pointing to their most dramatic features so readers can sense the issue topography.

Step 7. Eliminate nonspecific adverbs and adjectives. "Most," "significant" (unless used to discuss statistical results), "substantial," and scores of other adjectives may be decorative in the eyes of the writer, but they are obstacles to the reader. William Zinsser (1994) calls them "weasel words." They give the reader no specific idea about how the noun should be modified. Does a "large number of legislators" constitute a majority? A minority? Or two disaffected people? Could you count the "many instances in which the program failed" on one hand? Two hands? A calculator? Nouns and verbs should do the work themselves.

Step 8. Eliminate redundant words. Many words or phrases stick together like last night's spaghetti, when only one word is needed. Absolute necessity; active consideration; close proximity; conclusive proof; end result; free gift; general rule; old adage; proposed plan; past history; self-confessed; temporary reprieve; unsubstantiated rumor; green in color; large in size; plan in advance; filled to capacity; few in number; exactly the same; unless and until; completely surrounded; eliminate entirely; might possibly; mutually agreeable; assemble together; follow after; cancel out; merge together; termed as; visit with (Veniola, 1987, p. 68).

Step 9. Eliminate little qualifiers. Strunk and White (1979) call meaningless adjectival phrases such as "type of," "sort of," "kind of," "a little," "in a very real sense," "leeches that infest the pond of prose, sucking the blood from words" (p. 32). Eighteenth-century doctors used leeches only because they didn't understand their patients' illnesses or how to cure them but needed to do something.

RULE 8: AVOID JARGON

Part of the uniform of the expert is a new vocabulary. These new words or, worse, old words used in new ways may promote precise communication among experts. But this noble purpose is soon perverted. Technical language becomes jargon, confusing instead of clarifying. It excludes the uninitiated from debating technical issues. Academic journals—the expert's route to tenure and professional respect—elevate jargon into orthodoxy. To be published, the expert must use special words, bow before a pantheon of accepted works, and ignore the nonexpert. But technical words are chosen by our profession, not by the reader's. Using them erects barriers between writer and reader.

Government and business bureaucrats have their own languages for similar rituals. The writing expert Richard Mitchell (1979) suggests,

> One of the most important uses of language in all cultures is the performance of magic. . . . Wherever language exists, it is used in the attempt to constrain, or appease, or flatter, or beseech the spirit world. Typically, the language of incantation is oblique and arcane, always distinguished in some formal way from the language of everyday speech. The gods and spirits are ordinarily not addressed by name, unless you really have their numbers and can command them, and the benefits sought are usually phrased in delicate euphemisms and contrived circumlocutions. There are also, in all languages, certain magical words, words not common in the daily lexicon and sometimes known only to the initiated few. If you know these words, you can at least compel the attention of the spirits. For any speaker of a language, its use displays his license of membership in the culture and elicits from other members whatever is included in the list of privileges and benefits, but a more special form of the language can admit him to inner circles. We have no more confidence in the priests, but that is by no means to say that we have no more confidence in magic. We have simply consecrated new priests to its service. . . . Many of these priests are professors. They have learned their lore and lingo in our colleges and universities, and there they lurk. (pp. 113-114)

Using jargon may have an even more insidious result. It makes us less human. We can name things without conjuring a mental picture of them. In a powerful essay, "Politics and the English Language," George Orwell argues

> Millions of peasants are robbed of their farms and sent trudging along the roads with no more than they can carry: this is called "transfer of population," or "rectification of frontiers." People are imprisoned for years without trial, or shot in the back of the neck: this is called "elimination of the undesirable elements." (quoted in Zinsser, 1994, p. 15)

Public agencies often describe their mission as "providing assistance to" their clients, not "helping" them. Helping sounds too direct. Notice that it is also passive. As a result, these agencies report each year how much "assistance has been provided": They might list the number of training programs provided to poor people, how many people received advice on nutrition, and other measures of what an agency accomplished. But since they do not regard their task as helping their clients—to find a job, or live more healthy lives, for example—they conceal the futility of their efforts. "Providing assistance" suggests that their first duty is to the accountants who will provide money for the program based on the number of people receiving assistance. The clients, on the other hand, who want, and would be grateful for, help, are placed second. Words matter.

Journalese is a special strain of jargon, a quilt of instant words patched together out of other parts of speech. Adjectives are used as nouns ("greats"); nouns are used as adjectives ("health reasons") or extended into adjectives ("insightful"). Nouns are used as verbs ("to host") or chopped off into verb forms ("to put teeth into"). Technical reports often lapse into journalese, an attempt to lighten dense prose. The effect is a verbal tic—sodden technical language interrupted by inappropriate words.

Avoid jargon by seeking the right word instead of relying on the familiar one. Ask, do I know what this word means and suggests? Do I know what its hooks are for linking with other words? Read over one of your paragraphs. Does it sound like you speaking? Are the words the same you would say to a friend as you explained what you do at work? If not, you have lost direct contact with the reader. Soon, the reader will put aside your writing and turn to something more engaging.

Each of us is vulnerable to a handful of jargon words imprinted through training and habit. Read over some of your past papers. Write out the jargon words and phrases and pin them above the desk. When you have finished writing, search what you've written for each occurrence of your jargon (word processors make this easy). Rewrite to eliminate them if you can. Those instances that remain will, at least, have had to fight for their existence.

Step 1. Omit vague vogue words such as "interface," "utilize," "concept," "structure," "parameter," "function," "implement," and "hypothesize." If the writer selected words based on what is fashionable, the reader fears, perhaps he or she selected ideas based on their trendiness rather than soundness. Don't be pompous. Prefer "let" to "permit," "buy" to "purchase," "people" to "persons" or "individuals," "many" to "numerous," and "enough" to "sufficient." However technical the subject, we should use the same words in our writing that we use in everyday language.

Step 2. Never use a simile or metaphor, slang, or euphemisms commonly seen in print. We are often tempted to brighten technical writing with familiar phrases: "The implementation of the program illustrated the old adage that too many cooks spoil the broth." Or "The budget deficit has trapped the agency between a rock and a hard place." But old adages don't help readers see issues in new ways. If we are confident in our analyses, we want to convey our thoughts, and the best way to do this is to make all words entirely our own.

AFTERWORD

Break any rule if it will help decision makers understand you better. At all times, remember we write to help the reader—not to demonstrate our expertise or diligence or, worst of all, to be right. Every aspect of writing— from the choice of title to paragraph structure, selection of words, and punctuation should be selected for the reader—to make easier the difficult task of converting words into understanding.

SUMMARY

Policy analysts who effectively communicate with decision makers always follow this strategy: Keep it short; make it clear; tell a story; and rewrite, rewrite, and rewrite.

References

Advisory Commission on Intergovernmental Relations. (1996). *Intergovernmental Accountability* (SR-21). Washington, DC: Author.

All things considered. (1998, Jan. 7). National Public Radio.

Alonzo, W., & Starr, P. (1987). *The politics of numbers.* New York: Russell Sage.

Amacher, R., & Ulbrich, H. H. (1986). *Principles of economics.* Cincinnati, OH: South-Western Publications.

America extrapolated. (1992, January 3). *The Economist,* pp. 25-27.

American growth. (1992, December 26). *The Economist,* p. 91.

Andreski, S. (1972). *Social science as sorcery.* London: Andre Deutsch.

Apogee Associates. (1987). *Waste water treatment.* Washington, DC: National Council on Public Works Improvement.

Barnekov, T., & Hart, D. (1993). The changing nature of U.S. urban policy evaluation. *Urban Studies, 309,* 1469-1483.

Barr, S. (1997, June 3). Agencies are having difficulty. *Washington Post,* p. A17.

Behn, R. D. (1981). Policy analysis and public management. In G. S. Birkhead & J. D. Carroll (Eds.), *Education for public service.* Syracuse, NY: Maxwell School of Citizenship.

Bell, D., & Kristol, I. (Eds.). (1981). *The crisis in economic theory.* New York: Basic Books.

Bennett, W. (1988). *American education.* Washington, DC: U.S. Department of Education.

Beyle, T. L., & Muchmore, L. R. (1983). *Being governor: The view from the office.* Durham, NC: Duke University Press.

Bleakley, F. R. (1997, March 25). Some economic forecasts may be biased. *Wall Street Journal,* p. A3.

Bonnett, T. (1994). *New vocabulary for governing in the 1990s.* Washington, DC: Council of Governors' Policy Advisors.

Boulding, K. E. (1966a). *Economic analysis.* New York: Harper & Row.

Boulding, K. E. (1966b). *The impact of the social sciences.* New Brunswick, NJ: Rutgers University Press.

Brandl, J. E. (1985). Distilling frenzy from academic scribbling. *Journal of Public Policy and Management, 5,* 344-353.

Bryan, C. S. (1997). *Osler: Inspirations from a great physician.* New York: Oxford University Press.

Buss, T. F., & Gemmel, D. (1994). *Entrepreneurship in the Upper Peninsula.* Michigan Department of Economic Development.

Buss, T. F., & Redburn, F. S. (1983). *Shutdown at Youngstown.* Albany: State University of New York Press.

Buss, T. F., & Redburn, F. S. (1986). *Hidden unemployment*. New York: Praeger.

Buss, T. F., & Vaughan, R. J. (1988). *On the rebound*. Washington, DC: Council of Governors' Policy Advisors.

Buss, T. F., & Vaughan, R. J. (1989, Winter). Misrepresenting health and human service agency caseload data. *Journal of Health and Human Resource Administration, 11,* 324-351.

Cairncross, A. (1971). *Essays in economic management*. London: George Allen & Unwin.

Cairncross, A. (1982). Economics in theory and practice. *American Economic Review,* Papers and Proceedings, 1-20.

Case, K. (1989). *Housing*. Washington, DC: Council of State Planning Agencies.

Chait, J. (1998, January 19). Reform placebo. *The New Republic,* pp. 15-16.

Chamfort, S. (1966). *Maximes par Chamfort*. Paris: Tchou. (Original work published 1805)

Chenyoweth, J. (1995). *A guide to community-based, collaborative strategic planning*. Washington, DC: Council of Governors' Policy Advisors.

Chinese puzzles. (1993, May 15). *The Economist,* p. 83.

Clines, F. K. (1998, January 25). Washington ellipse: Words of denial, carefully chosen. *New York Times,* p. 10.

Clower, R. (1995). *Economic doctrine and method*. London: Aldershot.

Coase, R. H. (1960, October). The problem of social costs. *Journal of Law and Economics, 3,* 1-44.

Coase, R. H. (1974, October). The lighthouse in economics. *Journal of Law and Economics, 17,* 357-376.

Colander, D. (1991, November). Economists don't teach students what they need to know. *Chronicle of Higher Education,* p. A52.

Cook, L. (1993). *Strategic policy for the nation's governors*. Washington, DC: Council of Governors' Policy Advisors.

Cook, L., Osterholt, J., & Riley, E. (1988). Anticipating tomorrow's issues. Washington, DC: Council of State Planning Agencies.

Corruption's price. (1998, January 14). *Wall Street Journal,* p. A18.

Courant, P. (1994, December). How would you know a good economic development policy if you tripped over one? *National Tax Journal, 47,* 863-881.

Cruze, A., et al. (1985). *Evaluation of industry and occupational employment projections*. Washington, DC: Bureau of Labor Statistics.

Darby, M. R. (1992). *Causes of declining growth*. Kansas City: Federal Reserve Bank of Kansas.

DeHaven-Smith, L. (1988). *Philosophical critiques of policy analysis*. Gainsville: University of Florida Press.

De Tocqueville, A. (1848). *Democracy in America* (Vol. 1). New York: Pratt, Woodford.

Devolution goes on devolving. (1998, January 3). *The Economist,* p. 25.

Drucker, P. F. (1964). *Managing for results*. New York: Harper & Row.

East, Asia: Which way to safety. (1998, January 10). *The Economist,* pp. 62-63.

Economic policy advice. (1985, January 24). *The Economist,* pp. 10-11.

Enthoven, A. C. (1974). Ten practical principles for policy and program analysis. In R. Zeckhauser (Ed.), *Cost benefit and policy analysis annual*. Chicago: Aldine.

Feyerabend, P. (1993). *Against method*. London: Verso.

Fraatz, J. M. (1983). Policy analysts as advocates. *Journal of Policy Analysis and Management, 12,* 273-276.

Frankel, C. (1973). The nature and sources of irrationalism. *Science, 180,* 927-931.

Frey, B., & Eichenberger, R. (1993, Fall). American and European economics and economists. *Journal of Economic Perspectives,* pp. 185-193.

Friedman, M. (1997, December 31). Asian values. *National Review,* pp. 36-37.

Frumkin, N. (1987). *Tracking America's economy.* New York: M. E. Sharpe.

Galbraith, J. K. (1978, March). Writing, typing and economics. *Atlantic Monthly,* pp. 102-105.

General Accounting Office. (1986). *Hunger counties* (PEMD-86-7BR). Washington, DC: Author.

General Accounting Office. (1994a, July). *Jobs and JTPA* (HEHS-94-177). Washington, DC: Author.

General Accounting Office. (1994b, March). *Multiple employment training programs* (HEHS-94-88). Washington, DC: Author.

General Accounting Office. (1994c, July 27). *SBA cannot assess success of its minority business programs* (T-RCED-94-278). Washington, DC: Author.

General Accounting Office. (1995, August). *Program evaluation* (PEMD-95-1). Washington, DC: Author.

General Accounting Office. (1996a, December). *Community development* (RCED-97-1). Washington, DC: Author.

General Accounting Office. (1996b, April). *Economic development: Limited information exists on impact of assistance provided by three agencies* (RCED-96-103). Washington, DC: Author.

General Accounting Office. (1998, November). *Federal education funding* (HEHS-98-46). Washington, DC: Author.

Georgoff, D. M., & Murdick, R. G. (1986, January/February). Manager's guide to forecasting. *Harvard Business Review,* pp. 110-124.

Goldhamer, H. (1978). *The advisor.* New York: Elsevier.

Good, C. E. (1989). *Mightier than the sword.* Charlottesville, NC: Blue Jeans Press.

Goodman, J. C., & Matthews, M. (1998, January 14). Clinton's proposal would expand Medicare's problems. *Wall Street Journal,* p. A18.

Gore, A. (1993). Creating a government that works better and costs less: The report of the National Performance Review. Washington, DC: National Performance Review.

Gramlich, E. (1981). *Benefit-cost analysis of government programs.* Englewood Cliffs, NJ: Prentice Hall.

Gravelle, J. (1992). *Enterprise zone: The design of tax incentives.* Congressional Research Service, Library of Congress.

Gravelle, J., Kiefer, D., & Zimmerman, D. (1992). *Is job creation a meaningful policy justification?* (CRS 9-697). Washington, DC: Congressional Research Service, Library of Congress.

Hahn, R. W., & Litan, R. E. (1997, July 30). Putting regulations to a test. *Washington Post,* p. A27.

Halperin, M. H. (1974). *Bureaucratic politics and foreign policy.* Washington, DC: Brookings Institution.

Halpert, R. (1990, October). On writing for reading. *Southern Medical Journal, 83*(10), 1118-1119.

Hamilton, L. H. (1992, Summer). Economists as public policy advisors. *Journal of Economic Perspectives, 6,*(3), 61-64.

Hansen, W. L. (1991, September). The education and training of economics doctorates. *Journal of Economic Literature,* pp. 1054-1087.

Hawkins, R. G., Ritter, L. S., & Walter, I. (1973, September). What economists think of their journals. *Journal of Economics Literature*, pp. 1088-1109.

Heyne, P. T. (1973). *The economic way of thinking*. Chicago: Science Research Associates.

Hibbert, C. (1997). *Wellington*. Reading, PA: Addison-Wesley.

How subsidies destroy the land. (1997, December 13). *The Economist*, pp. 21-22.

Huff, D. (1954). *How to lie with statistics*. New York: Norton.

Irland, L. C., Cogan, C. S., & Lawton, C. T. (1984, Fall). Forecasting a state's economy. *Northeast Journal of Business and Economics*, 2(1), 20-31.

Israel, L. (1982). *Decision-making: The modern doctor's dilemma*. New York: Random House.

Jay, A., & Lynn, J. (1981). *Yes Minister*. BBC TV.

Johnson, K., Frazier, W., & Riddick, M. (1983). A change strategy for linking the worlds of academia and practice. *Journal of Applied Behavioral Science, 19,* 439-460.

Junk science. (1994, October 24). *National Review*, pp. 22-24.

Kane, E. (1989, Fall). The high cost of incompletely funding FSLIC. *Journal of Economic Perspectives*, pp. 33-45.

Kaplan, A. (1964). *Conduct of inquiry*. San Francisco: Chandler.

Kaufman, G. G. (1995, Summer). The role of economists in public policy. *Quarterly Review of Economics and Finance, 35*(2), 177-185.

Kaus, M. (1991, May 20). Facts for hacks. *New Republic*, pp. 23-26.

Kaus, M. (1992, February 15). Thinking of Hillary. *New Republic*, pp. 6-12.

Keynes, J. M. (1919). *Economic consequences of the peace*. London: Penguin.

Keynes, J. M. (1933). *Essays in persuasion*. London: Macmillan.

Kingdon, J. W. (1986). *Congressmen's voting decisions* (3rd ed.). New York: Harper & Row.

Kitcher, P. (1985). *Vaulting ambition*. Cambridge: MIT Press.

Kornai, J. (1983). The health of nations. *Kyklos, 36,* 199-215.

Krieger, M. H. (1988). The inner game of writing. *Journal of Public Policy and Management, 8,* 56-61.

Krikelas, A. C. (1992, July/August). Why regions grow. *Federal Reserve Bank of Atlanta Economic Review, 77,* 16-29.

Krimerman, L. I. (1969). *The nature and scope of social science*. New York: Appleton-Century-Crofts.

Krugman, P. (1994). *The age of diminishing expectations*. Cambridge: MIT Press.

Krugman, P. (1996). *Pop internationalism*. Cambridge: MIT Press.

Kupfersmid, J. (1988). Improving what is published. *American Psychological Review, 43,* 635-642.

Lacker, J. M. (1994, Winter). Does adverse selection justify government intervention in loan markets? *Federal Reserve Bank of Richmond Economic Quarterly, 80,* 61-95.

Ladd, H. F. (1994). Spatially targeted economic development: Does it work? *Cityscape, 4,* 193-218.

Laffer, A. B. (1996, October 15). Creating wealth, not just savings. *Wall Street Journal*, p. A10.

Lasswell, H. (1971). *A preview of policy sciences*. New York: Elsevier.

Lawrence, J., & Bergman, E. M. (1985). *Research memorandum*. Research Triangle, NC: Research Triangle Institute.

Leahy, P., Buss, T. F., & Quane, J. (1996, January). Time on welfare. *American Journal of Economics and Sociology, 54,* 33-46.

Leman, C. K., & Nelson, R. H. (1981). Ten commandments for policy economists. *Journal of Public Policy and Analysis, 1,* 97-117.

Lin, X., Buss, T. F., & Popovich, M. (1990, August). Rural entrepreneurship is alive and well. *Economic Development Quarterly, 4,* 254-259.

Lindsey, D. (1977). Participation and influence in publication review. *American Psychological Review, 32,* 25-35.

Lynn, L. E. (1978). *Knowledge and policy: The uncertain connection.* Boston: Little, Brown.

MacRae, D., & Whittington, D. (1997). *Expert advice for policy choice.* Washington, DC: Georgetown University Press.

Maier, M. H. (1991). *The data game.* New York: M. E. Sharpe.

Majchrzak, A. (1984). *Methods for policy research.* Beverly Hills, CA: Sage.

Mannheim, K. (1941). *Man and society in an age of reconstruction.* New York: Harcourt Brace.

Manzullo, D. (1996, March 10). The Cliff Notes congress. *Wall Street Journal,* p. A10.

Maraniss, D. (1996, August 4). Meeting time. *Washington Post,* p. 10.

McCloskey, D. N. (1985a). Economical writing. *Economic Inquiry, 23,* 187-222.

McCloskey, D. N. (1985b). *The rhetoric of economics.* Madison: University of Wisconsin Press.

McCloskey, D. N. (1990). *If you're so smart.* Chicago: University of Chicago Press.

McGee, S. (1998, January 5). Debating the value of stock forecasts for 1998. *Wall Street Journal,* pp. C1-C2.

Meier, K. J. (1984). The limits of cost benefit analysis. In L. G. Nigro (Ed.), *Decision-making in the public sector.* New York: Marcel Dekker.

Meltsner, A. J. (1976). *Policy analysis in the bureaucracy.* Berkeley: University of California Press.

Micklewait, J., & Wooldridge, A. (1996). *The witch doctors.* New York: Random House.

Miller, J. (1978). *The body in question.* New York: Harper & Row.

Mills, C. W. (1961). *The sociological imagination.* New York: Grove.

Mills, E. (1993, Spring/Summer). The misuse of regional economic models. *Cato Journal, 13,* 29-38.

Mitchell, R. (1979). *Less than words can say.* New York: Little, Brown.

Musgrave, R. A., & Musgrave, P. B. (1990). *Public finance in theory and practice.* New York: McGraw-Hill.

Nagel, E. (1961). *The structure of science.* New York: Harcourt Brace.

Neustadt, K. J., & May, E. R. (1986). *Thinking in time.* New York: Free Press.

Nothdurft, W. (1988, September). Ten rules for marketing ideas. *Entrepreneurial Economy Review, 7,* 1-5.

Oregon Progress Board. (1982). *Oregon benchmarks.* Eugene: OR: Author.

Olson, M. (1965). *Logic of collective action.* Cambridge, MA: Harvard University Press.

Osborne, D., & Gaebler, T. (1992). *Reinventing government.* Reading, MA: Addison-Wesley.

Osborne, D., & Plastrik, P. (1997). *Banishing bureaucracy.* Reading, MA: Addison-Wesley.

The overlooked housekeeper. (1994. February 5). *The Economist,* p. 25.

Patton, G. S. (1974). *The Patton papers. Vol. 2: 1940-1945.* Boston: Houghton Mifflin.

Pedhazur, E., & Schmelkin, L. P. (1991). *Measurement, design, and analysis.* Hillsdale, NJ: Lawrence Erlbaum.

Plenty of gloom. (1997, December 20). *The Economist,* pp. 14-21.

Pollot, M. L. (1993). *Grand theft and petit larceny.* San Francisco: Pacific Research Institute.

RAND Corporation. (1975). *Target growth industries for New York City.* New York: Author.

RAND Corporation, (1983). *Target growth for New York City: A follow-up study.* New York: Author.

Redburn, F. S., & Buss, T. F. (1984). Religious leaders and the politics of revitalization. In R. Eyestone (Ed.), *Policy policy formation.* Greenwich, CO: JAI.

Redburn, F. S., & Buss, T. F. (1986). *Responding to America's homeless.* New York: Praeger.

Rhoads, S. E. (1978, March/April). Economists and policy analysis. *Public Administration Review,* pp. 112-119.

Rhoads, S. E. (1985). *An economist's view of the world.* Cambridge, UK: Cambridge University Press.

Ricardo, D. (1819). *On the principles of political economy.* Washington, DC: J. Milligan.

Ripley, R. B. (1985). *Policy analysis in political science.* Chicago: Nelson-Hall.

Rivlin, A. M. (1971). *Systematic thinking for social action.* Washington, DC: Brookings Institution.

Rubenstein, E. S. (1994). *The right data.* New York: National Review.

Rubin, M. (1994, March/April). Can reorchestration of historical themes reinvent government? *Public Administration Review, 54*(2), 161-169.

Sabatier, P. (1978, September). Acquisition and utilization of technical information by administrative agencies. *Administrative Science Quarterly, 23,* 396-417.

Safire, W. (1998, January 25). Rules of thumb. *New York Times Magazine,* p. 12.

Schon, D. A. (1983). *The reflective practitioner.* New York: Basic Books.

Scriven, M. (1983). The evaluation taboo. In E. R. House (Ed.), *Philosophy of evaluation.* San Francisco: Jossey-Bass.

Seelye, K. Q. (1998, January 8). President plans on $21 billion for child care. *New York Times,* p. A1.

Simon, H. (1981). *Sciences of the artificial.* Cambridge, MA: MIT Press.

Size isn't everything. (1998, January 31). *The Economist,* p. 60.

Sjoberg, L. (1982, October/December). Aided and unaided decision-making. *Journal of Forecasting,* pp. 349-359.

Smelser, N. J., & Gerstein, D. R. (Eds.). (1986). *Behavioral and social sciences: 50 years of discovery.* Washington, DC: National Academy Press.

South Carolina Legislature. (1985). *A review of state's economic development activities.* Legislative Audit Council, South Carolina Legislature.

Sowell, T. (1996). *Knowledge and decisions.* New York: Basic Books.

Squire, L., & van der Tak, H. G. (1975). *Economic project analysis.* Baltimore: Johns Hopkins University Press.

State Planning Office. (1983). *Minnesota milestones.* Minneapolis, MN: Office of the Governor, State Planning Office.

Stigler, G. J. (1984). *The intellectual in the marketplace.* Cambridge, MA: Harvard University Press.

Stigler, G. J. (1988). *Memoirs of an unregulated economist.* New York: Basic Books.

Stiglitz, J. E. (1988). *Economics of the public sector.* New York: Norton.

Stinchcombe, A. L. (1968). *Constructing social theories.* New York: Harcourt Brace & World.

Stockman, D. (1983). *The triumph of politics.* New York: Random House.

Storer, N. W. (1966). *The social system of science.* New York: Holt, Rinehart & Winston.

Stouffer, S. A. (1950). Some observations on study design. *American Journal of Sociology, 55,* 355-361.

Strunk, W., & White, E. B. (1979). *Elements of style* (3rd ed.). Boston: Allyn & Bacon.

Sy, K. J. (1987). University-state linkages revisited. *Policy Studies Journal, 16*(1), 3-26.

Sylvia, R. D., Sylvia, K. M., & Gunn, E. M. (1997). *Program planning and evaluation.* Prospect Heights, IL: Waveland.

Sypher, B. D., & Zorn, T. E. (1986, Spring). Communication-related abilities and upward mobility. *Human Communication Research,* pp. 420-431.

Thompson, W. (1972). *Preface to urban economics.* Baltimore: John Hopkins University Press.

Toulmin, S. (1958). *The uses of argument.* Cambridge, UK: Cambridge University Press.

Tukey, J. W. (1969). Analyzing data: Sanctification or detective work? *American Psychological Review, 24,* 83-91.

Ulmer, M. J. (1984, November). Economics in decline. *Commentary,* pp. 42-46.

Vaughan, R. J. (1980). *Inflation and unemployment.* Washington, DC: Council of State Planning Agencies.

Vaughan, R. J., Pollard, R., & Dyer, B. (1984). *Wealth of states.* Washington, DC: Council of State Planning Agencies.

Veniola, J. (1987). *Rewrite right.* Berkeley, CA: Ten Speed Press.

Verdier, J. M. (1984). Advising congressional decision-makers. *Journal of Policy Analysis and Management, 4,* 421-438.

Ward, W., & Deren, B. (1991). *The economics of project analysis.* Washington, DC: World Bank.

Weimer, D. L., & Vining, A. R. (1992). *Policy analysis.* Englewood Cliffs, NJ: Prentice Hall.

Weinstein, M. (1990, April 5). Editorial notebook. *The New York Times,* p. A25.

Weiss, C. H. (1992). *Organizations for policy analysis.* Newbury Park, CA: Sage.

Weiwal, W., Persky, J., & Felsenstein, D. (1995, Fall). Are subsidies worth it? *Economic Development Commentary,* pp. 10-16.

Wessel, D. (1997, January 27). In setting Fed's policy, chairman bets heavily on his own judgement. *Wall Street Journal,* pp. A1, A5.

Whiteman, D. (1986). Fate of policy analysis in congressional decision-making. *Western Political Quarterly, 39,* 394-311.

Who's really who. (1998, January 3). *The Economist,* pp. 51-52.

Wildavsky, A. (1979). *Speaking truth to power: The art and craft of policy analysis.* Boston: Little, Brown.

Wildavsky, A., & Caiden, N. (1997). *The new politics of the budgetary process.* New York: Longman.

Winch, P. (1958). *The idea of a social science.* London: Routledge & Kegan Paul.

Yanow, D. (1996). *How does a policy mean?* Washington, DC: Georgetown University Press.

Zeckhauser, R. (1974). *Cost benefit and policy analysis annual.* Chicago: Aldine.

Zinsser, W. (1988). *Writing to learn.* New York: Harper & Row.

Zinsser, W. (1994). *On writing well* (5th ed.). New York: HarperCollins.

Index

Accountability, 3, 39, 94, 102, 105
Action-forcing events, 56
Advancement of Social Science Coalition, 1
Adverse selection, 62
Adverse side effects, 48
Advisory Council of Intergovernmental Relations (ACIR), 39
Aesthetic benefits, 35
Affordable housing, 8
Agency effects, 53
Agents, 63
Alabama Coalition Against Hunger, 19
Alabama Legislature, 101
Alcoholism treatment centers, 29
Alexander, Governor Lamar, 102
All Things Considered, 23
Alonzo, W., 15, 20
Amacher, R., 10, 43, 57
American Association of Retired People (AARP), 27
American Economic Review, 4
Andreski, S., 123
Apogee Associates, 15
Applied policy analysis, 5-13
Apprenticeship, 30
Arizona, 97
Asian banks, 9
Association or causal methods, 79, 81

Balance Agriculture with Industry Program, 113
Bank regulation, 36
Banks, 21, 30, 36, 40, 43, 44, 46, 86
    Asian, 9
Barnekov, T., 92
Barr, Joseph, 100, 114
Base, defined, 62

Behn, R. D., 1
Bell, Daniel, 118
Benchmark, 97, 104, 105
Benefits over costs, 65
Benefits, 59, 61
Bergman, E. M., 76
Best practice, 47
Beyle, Thad L., 14
Bleakley, F. R., 86
Body in Question, The, 30
Bonnett, Tom, 57
Boulding, Kenneth, 108, 132
Boxes, policy, 47
Brandl, John, 112, 118
Brookings Institute, 2
Bryan, C. S., 8, 11
Budget crisis, 56
Budget Enforcement Act of 1990, 64
Bureau of Reclamation, 59
Bureaucratic environment, 53
Bush, President George, 68
Business formation rate, 43
Buss, Terry F., 9, 15, 16, 26-28, 32, 34, 43, 52

Caiden, N. 62
Cairncross, Sir Alec, 38, 116
Carter, President Jimmy, 37
Cascade effect, 31
Case, K., 16
Causal links, 46
CBS Evening News, 18
Chait, J., 68
Chamfort, Sebastien, 107
Chenyoweth, J., 66
Child abuse, 29
Children's Services, 28
Citizens for Tax Justice, 114

Clean Water Act, 120
Clines, F. K., 109
Clinton, Hillary, 68
Clinton, President William Jefferson, 2,
    68-69, 115, 137
Closely held issues, 57
Clower, Robert, xi, 4, 84, 120
Coase, R. H., 36, 63
Cogan, C. S., 82
Colander, David, 4
Communication, 12, 98
Communication strategy, 68
Community health center, 20
Community mental health center, 28
Compensation, 62
Competition, 9, 14, 21, 63
Comprehensive Employment and Training
    Partnership Act (CETA), 98
Compromise, 41
Conditional initiatives, 54
Conflict resolution, 41
Conflicts in values, 41
Congress, 3, 16, 23, 37, 59, 64, 112, 128
Congressional Budget Office (CBO), 22,
    25, 116
Congressmen's voting decisions, 54
Connecticut Product Development Corpora-
    tion, 46
Consensus, 41, 52, 86
Construction jobs as benefits, 59-60
Consulting, 19, 22, 78-79
Consumer Price Index (CPI), 115
Consumption, 111
Context of discovery, 47
Context of explanation, 47
Contradicting policy goals, 64
Convention center, 62
Cook, Lauren, 55, 70, 83
Corruption, 38
Cost and benefits, 11, 47-48, 50-51, 59-60,
    63-66, 71-72, 92
Cost-benefit and policy analysis, 6-7
Council of State Policy and Planning Agen-
    cies, 43
Countercyclical policies, 49
Counting methods, 79-80
Courant, P., 64
Cowperthwaite, John, 9
Creaming, 99, 101

Cruze, A. 84
Cultural amenities, 35

Dairy price supports, 10
Darby, M. R., 21
DDT, 77
Decentralized, 63, 102
Decision making, 92
Decision-Making: The Modern Doctor's Di-
    lemma, 45
Define, 43
DeHaven-Smith, L., xi
Delegation of authority, 63
Democracy in America, 25
Deniability, 109
Department of Economic Security, 97
Deregulation of interstate freight, 21
Deren, B., 6, 34, 67
Developmentally disabled, 100
Devolution, 63
Diagnoses, 9, 26
Diagnostics, 9-10
Discount rate, 65
Discounting for risks, 66
Discouraged workers, 20, 32
Displaced workers, 20, 27, 30, 41, 94, 96
Disraeli, Benjamin, 19, 68
Distributional effects, 64
Diversification, 64
Drucker, Peter, 94
Duke of Wellington (Arthur Wellesley), 19
Dyer, Barbara, 23

Econometric, 3
Economic way of thinking, 118
Economist, The, 3, 31, 130
Education, 8, 26, 38, 40, 49, 58-59, 78, 93,
    99
Efficacy, 69
Efficiency, 64, 92, 102, 116-117
Eichenberger, R., xi-xii, 12
Eisenhower, President Dwight, 22
Electoral process, 14
Electricity, 79
Emergency room, 14, 31
Eminent domain, 62
Employment services, 29

Empowerment zones, 67
Energy prices, 37
Energy, 36-37, 46
Enterprise zone, 64, 67, 96
Enthoven, Alain, 12, 19, 107
Entrepreneurs, 43-44
Environment laws, 36, 66
   Policy, 1
   Pollution, 33
Environmental Protection Agency (EPA), 49
Equal Rights Amendment (ERA), 35
Equity, 116, 120
Essays in Economic Management (Cairn-
   cross), 38
Etiology, 8
Evaluation, 11-12, 41, 46, 48, 59, 61, 70,
   76, 102
Executive orders, 54
Experiment, 93, 102
Expiration dates, 23
Externalities, 34-36

Fact-check, 40
Factoids, 15-18
Facts, nature of, 15
Farm subsidy, 20
Federal Bureau of Investigation (FBI), 28
Federal Highway Administration, 119
Federal Reserve Bank, 75, 86
Federal Reserve Board, 23
Felsentein, D., 60
Feyerabend, Paul, xi
Fiscal flow analysis, 60
Florida, 105
Food Research and Action Center, 18
Food subsidies, 19
Forecast data, 85
Ford, President Gerald, 8
Forecasting, 75-92
Forecasting linearity, 87
   Techniques, 79-81
   Turning points, 87
Fraatz, J. M., 116
Frankel, C., 3
Fraud and abuse, 120
Frazier, W., 2
Free trade, 120
Frey, B., xi-xii, 12

Friedman, Milton, 8, 68
Frumkin, N., 20, 25

Gaebler, T., 63, 125
Galbraith, John Kenneth, 123
Galileo's Dialogo, 122
Game, as technique, 99
Gemmel, D., 34
General Accounting Office (GAO), 19, 46,
   92, 99
General Education Diploma (GED), 99
General Motors, 22
Georgoff, David M., 76, 79, 83
Gerstein, D. R., 3
GI Bill, 26
Goal conflict, 64
Goals, 95
Goldhamer, H., x-xi, 1-2
Good, C. E., 139
Goodman, J. C., 68
Gore, Vice President Al, 120
Government as beneficiary, 60
   Failure, 67
   Intervention, 38
Government Performance Act, 100
Graham, Governor Bob, 102-103, 105-106
Gramlich, E., 65
Gravelle, J., 64
Greenspan, Alan, 23, 75
Gross domestic product (GDP), 81
Gunn, E. M., 79

Hahn, R. W., 25
Halperin, M. H., 56
Halpert, R., 12, 122
Hamilton, Lee, x-xii, 1, 3-5, 108-109, 113,
   123
Hard Heads, Soft Hearts (Binder), 5
Hart, 92
Hawkins, R. G, 4
Health insurance, 68
Heyne, Paul T., 6, 44
Hibbert, C., 19
Hidden costs, 118
High technology, 23
Highway link, 72
Hippocratic oath, 11
Historical analogies, 26, 37

History, importance of, 25-27
Holmes, Sherlock, 15
Home mortgage, 16
Homeless, 9, 10, 14, 16-17, 33
Hong Kong, 8
Housing, 3, 16, 18, 33, 87
Housing and Urban Development (HUD), 16
How to Lie with Statistics (Huff), 22
Huff, Darrell, 22-23
Hugo, Victor, 28
Human service agencies, 16, 78, 101
Hypotheses, 31-32, 40-44

Immigration, 3
Incentives, 35, 63, 98, 99, 102, 118-119
Indiana, 101
Indirect consequences, 120
Industrial park, 62
Inflation, 32
Inner city, 34, 52, 67
Innovation, 46
Input, 93
Intended consequences, 92
Internal rate of return, 64-65
Internationalized, 36
Intervention, 46, 52, 63-64, 67, 104
Investment, 111
Irland, L. C., 82
Israel, Lucien, M.D., 45
Issue treatment file, 103

Japan, 9
Jargon, 123
Jay, Antony, 57
Jefferson, President Thomas, 122
Job search assistance, 40
Job Training Partnership Act (JTPA), 98-99
Johnson, K., 2
Joint Econmic Committee, 123
Jong, Erica, 131
Journalese, 141
Judgment, 79-83
"Junk Science," 1

Kane, Ed, 110
Kaplan, Abraham, 8, 17
Kaufman, G. G., x-xii, 1-2, 4-5

Kaus, Mickey, 18, 22
Keifer, Donald, 64
Kentucky, 58
Keynes, John Maynard, 5, 75, 103
Keyserling, Leon, 108
Kingdon, John, 53-54
KISS principle, 110
Kitcher, P., 12
Kornai, Janos, 47-48
Kraft General Foods, 19
Kraus, Karl, 124
Krieger, Martin, 124, 126
Krikelas, A. C., 89
Krimerman, L. I., 3
Kristol, Irving, 118
Krugman, Paul 20
Kupfersmid, J., 4

Lacker, J. M., 63
Ladd, Helen F., 64
Laffer, A. B., 60
Laid-off workers, 29
Language, 123, 127, 141
Lasswell, Harold, 12, 31
Latino, 17
Lawrence, J., 76
Lawton, C. T., 82
Lawyers, 4
Leahy, Peter, 26
Legislative agenda, 55
Leman, Christopher, 56, 111, 116
Lemming instinct, 32
Lighthouses, 63
Lin, Xiannan, 43
Lindsey, D., 4
Litan, R. E., 25
Loans, 43-44, 52
Log rolling, 56
London, 24
Lynn, Lawrence E., 3
Lynn, Jonathan, 57

McDonalds Restaurant, 21
MacNamara, Robert, 19
MacRae, Donald, xi, 6, 9, 51
Maier, M. H., 20, 25
Mailer, Norman, 125
Maine, 82

Majchrzak, Ann, x, 69
Malfeasance, 39
Malpractice insurance, 32
Man and Society in an Age of Reconstruction, 2
Mannheim, Karl, 2
Manzullo, D., 132
Maraniss, D., 122, 132
Marginalism, 111
Market failure, 63
Market failure, 67
Marshall, Alfred, 44
Marx, Karl, 2, 112
Massachusetts, 4
Matthews, M., 68
May, Ernest, 26, 37
McCloskey, Donald, xi., 3, 5, 12, ,37, 122, 125, 127, 129
McGee, S., 4
McGovern, Senator George, 68
McIntire, Robert, 114
McKinney Act, 18
Meachem, Governor Evan (AZ), 97
Meals on Wheels, 117
Medicaid, 61, 68
Medicaid/Medicare fraud, 33
Medical decision-making protocols, 75
Medicare, 68
Meltsner, A. J., 56
Meyler's Side Effects of Drugs, 47
Michigan, 34
Micklewait, J., 102
Miller, Jonathan, 30, 69, 113
Mills, C. Wright, 89, 128
Mining, 118
Minnesota, 104, 112, 118
Minnesota Milestones, 105
Minorities, 35
Mississippi, 113
Missouri Legislature, 101
Misuse of terms, 57
Massachusetts Institute of Technology (MIT), 2
Mitchell, Richard, 123, 141
Model, 2-3, 11, 69, 75-76
Model cities, 67
Mortality, 24
Moynihan, Senator Daniel Patrick, 22
Muchmore, Lynn, 14

Multiplier effect, 111
Murdick, Robert G., 76, 79, 83
Murphy's law, 5
Musgrave, Patricia B., 34
Musgrave, Robert A., 34

Nabokov, Vladimir, 125
Nagel, Ernest, 8
National Academy of Public Administration (NAPA), 39
National Center for Research, 19
Negative income tax, 68
Negotiation, 106, 110
Nelson, Robert, 56, 111, 116
Net present value, 64-65
Neustadt, K. J., 37
New Jersey, 119
New Republic, 18
New York, 119
New York Times, 56, 112, 115
Nonsystemic problems, 39-40
Normative economics, 116
North American Free Trade Agreement (NAFTA), 3
Northdurft, William, 17
Northern Arizona University, 97, 101
Nuestadt, Richard, 26, 56
Nutter, Warren G., 1

Objective, 95
Office of Budget and Management (OBM), 86
Ohio, 57, 86
Ohio State University (OSU), 87
Oil, 24, 37, 42-43
Olson, M., 10
Op-Ed, 122, 131
Opportunity, 6, 58, 60
Opportunity costs, 59-61, 110-111
Optimizing models, 117
Oregon, 61, 104-105
Oregon Progress Board, 104
Organization of Petroleum Exporting Countries (OPEC), 8, 24, 37
Orwell, George, 141
Osborne, David, 63, 125
Osler, Sir William, 8, 11

Osterholt, J., 70
Outcome, 46, 48, 51, 59, 51, 66, 70-72, 75, 83, 93, 99, 104, 106
Output, 93, 104

Package policy analysis, 5
Parental choice, 58
Parliament, 24
Partial analysis, 56
Patient's bill of rights, 68
Patton, General George S., 98
Pedhazur, E., 2, 47, 85
Performance measurement, 93, 95, 97, 99-101, 103
Performance, 39, 92, 94, 98
Persky, J., 60
Pilot projects, 40
Placebos, 58, 70
Planning, 76
Planning and forecasting, 77
Plant closing, 15, 27, 33-37, 77, 120
Plastrik, P., 63
Police crime statistics, 28
Policy, 57
    Advocacy, 19, 116
    Analysis matrix, 33
    Cycle, 55
    Logo, 49
    Medicine and policy analysis compared, 7
    Portfolio, 52
    Priorities, 50
    Process, 55
    Timetable, 54
Pollard, Robert, 23
Pollot, M. L., 62
Pollution, environmental, 34-35, 61
Polypharmacy, 67
Popovich, Mark, 43
Popper, Karl, 125
Pork barrel, 54
Pornography, 112
Portfolio, policy, 52
Positive economics, 116
Prenatal care, 49
Prescription, 10-11
Prescription drugs, 55
Present value, 12

President Truman's Council of Economic Advisors, 108
Priorities, 50
Private and public actions, 33
Problem assessment, 14
Problem, diagnosing, 33, 43
Process, 3, 38, 41, 48, 52, 54, 66-67, 72, 112
Professional journals, 47, 131
Prognosis, 11-12
Psychiatric hospitals, 28
Public health clinics, 68
Public utilities, 79
Public works, 59, 119

Quane, James, 26
Quasi-autonomous non-governmental organizations (QANGOs), 63

RAND Corporation, 90
Raspberry, William, 22
Rather, Dan, 18
Reagan, President Ronald, 68, 113
Redburn, F. Stevens, 9, 15-16, 27, 32, 52
Redistribution, 60, 72
Reinventing Government (Osborne), 125
Relative risks, 51
Rent-seeking, defined, 10
Retraining, 32, 46
Rhoads, Steven E., 13, 61, 70-71, 111, 117
Ricardo, David, 115
Riddick, M., 2
Riley, E., 70
Ripley, Randall B., xi
Risk assessment, 66
Risk, 51, 65, 70
Ritter, L. S., 4
Rivlin, Alice M., 2, 3
Rolling out, 93
Rubenstein, E. S., 20
Rubin, M., 26
Rules for clear writing, 12
Rules of thumb, x
Rural development, 42
Rural strategy, 34

Sabatier, Paul, 1
Safire, William, x

Satisficing, 117
Scenarios, 70
Schmelkin, P., 2, 47, 85
Schon, Donald, 2-3
School choice, 58
Schultze, Charles, 116
Scriven, Michael, 8
Self-correcting mechanisms, 41
Shadow price, 59
Share, defined, 62
Side effects, 45
Signs, 8-9, 42
Simon, Herbert, 117
Sjoberg, L., 83
Small business, 14, 30, 34, 36, 40, 46, 92
    Loan subsidies, 31
Smelser, N. J., 3
Smith, Adam, 112
Smog, 24
Snyder, Mitch, 16
Social costs, 36
Social medicine, 68
Social science, xi, 2, 4, 11, 13, 23, 42, 47, 113
    Practice, ix-xii
    Social Science Citation Index, 4
Social scientists, xii, 5, 7, 25, 116-117
Social Security, 22, 42, 97
Social service, 18
Social welfare, 15, 27
South Carolina Legislature, 89
South Dakota, 101
South Korea, 9
Sowell, Thomas, 116
Spillovers, 35
Spin, 68
Squire, L., 6, 34
Stakeholders, 11, 52, 66, 120
Stamp, Sir Josiah, 20
Starr, P., 20, 25
Statistics, 19-21, 23-25, 41, 49, 56, 64, 75,
    112, 114
Steel industry, 30, 58
Stein, Herbert, 110
Stigler, George, xi, 24
Stiglitz, Joseph E., 62-63
Stinchcombe, A. L., 10, 31
Stock market, 9
Stock market forecasters, 4
Stockman, D., 27

Storer, N. W., 4
Stouffer, S. A., 4-5, 12
Strunk, William, 129, 140
Subsidies, 24, 64, 66, 118
Substance abuse, 9
Suburbs, 67
Sunk costs, 62
Supply side economics, 113
Swift, Jonathan, ix
Swine flu, 8
Sy, K. J., 2
Sylvia, K. M, 79
Sylvia, R. D., 79
Symptomatology, 8-9, 30
Symptoms, 8-9, 13, 30-31, 42-43
Sypher, B. D., 124
Systemic and nonsystemic problem, 33

Takings, 62
Targeted industries, 89
Task force, 11, 77
Tax incentive, 33
Taxes, 3, 10, 23, 36, 55-56, 60, 67-68, 72,
    76, 90, 119-120
Technology, 33, 52, 60
Teen pregnancies, 63, 104
Television, 114
Tennessee, 102
Tennessee Valley Authority, 102
Texas Legislature, 109
Theoretical construct, 113
Theory, x-xi, 4-5, 7, 13, 24-25, 112, 130
Thinking in Time (Neustadt & May), 26
Thompson, Wilbur, 60
Time magazine, 22
Timelines, 26
Time-series methods, 79-80
Timing, 57
Tocqueville, Alexis de, 25
Tornadoes, 50
Toulmin, Stephen, 1
Toxic waste, 36
Trade deficit, 21
Trade-off, 45, 102
Training Adjustment Act, 30
Training, 30, 46, 49, 54, 58, 70-71, 90, 96-99
Transfer payments, 20, 72
Transportation, 21

Triage, 50
Trump, Donald, 18
Tukey, William 24

UK Central Statistic Office, 19
UK Ministry of Health, 24
UK Prime Minister, 68
Ulbrich, H. H., 10, 34, 57
Ulmer, M. J., 3
Unemployment, 9, 14, 20, 50, 52, 60, 70, 79
Unemployment insurance, 29, 41,97
Unintended consequences, 36, 58, 111,
    118-120
United States Bureau of Labor Statistics
    (BLS), 32, 84, 97
United States Department of Agriculture, 79
United States Department of Commerce,
    21, 82
United States Forest Service, 111
United States Merit System Protection
    Board, 120
United States State Department, 56
Upper Peninsula, Michigan, 34
Urban Development Action Grant
    (UDAG), 40
Urban Institute, 72
User fees, 59

Value, 59-61, 72, 98, 100, 112, 109, 117
Value of life, 61
van der Tak, H. G., 6, 34
Vaughan, Roger J., 15-16, 23, 28, 31, 49,
    50, 60
Veniola, J., 140
Venture capital, 23, 49-50, 66
Verdier, James 25, 56, 108, 114, 116, 132
Vining, A. R., xi
Vocabulary, 53, 57, 70
Voodoo economics, 68-69
Voucher, 57-58

Walter, I., 4
Wall Street, 36
Wal-Mart, 41
Ward, W., 6, 34, 67
Washington Post, 56
Washington, D.C., 16, 39, 72
Waste disposal, 10, 33, 39
Wastewater, 15, 119
Watergate, 1
Watson, Dr. James, 15
Wealth, 60
Weimer, D. L., xi
Weinstein, Michael, 112
Weiss, Carol H., 5, 57
Weiwal, Wim, 60, 92
Welfare, 26, 29-30, 33, 40, 93
Wessel, D., 75
Wetland, 62
White, E. B., 129, 140
Whitehead, Alfred North, 123
Whiteman, D., x
Whittington, D., xi, 6, 9, 51
Wildavsky, Aaron, 1, 5, 62
Winch, Peter, 3
Winter, Governor William, 113-114
Wooldridge, A., 102
World War I, 75
World War II, 24, 26, 37

Yanow, David, 122, 124
Yerby, Frank, 125
Yes Minister, 57
Youngstown, Ohio, 15, 17, 27-30, 42, 52, 58

Zeckhauser, R., 19
Zero-based budgeting, 62
Zimmerman, Dennis, 64
Zinsser, William, 122-124, 128, 138, 140-141
Zorn, T. E., 124

About the Authors

Roger J. Vaughan heads his own consulting firm specializing in policy analysis for all levels of government. He earned a PhD in economics from the University of Chicago, an MA from McGill University, and a BA from Oxford University. He was a senior economist for Citicorp in New York, director of economic development for New York's Governor Carey, and senior policy fellow with the RAND Corporation and the Council of Governors' Policy Advisors (CGPA), an affiliate of the National Governors' Association in Washington, D.C. He has worked as a policy analyst for governors in over 30 states. He has written over 150 books and articles on public policy issues. He has also worked on national and local policies issues in Hungary, Bulgaria, Russia, and other newly independent states. For the past 3 years, he has worked in-country as a consultant with PADCO, Inc., offering technical assistance to the Cabinet of Ministers in the Ukraine.

Terry F. Buss is Professor and Chair of the Department of Public Management, Sawyer School of Business, at Suffolk University in Boston. He holds a PhD in political science and mathematics from Ohio State University. He has written over 200 professional publications on public policy issues ranging from human services management to economic development. Since 1991, he has worked in Hungary, Russia, Bulgaria, Romania, and Slovakia, assisting public officials in making the transition from communism to democracy. He received two separate Fulbright Fellowships, one at the Budapest University of Economic Sciences and the other at the Budapest School of Public Administration, where he offered technical assistance to local governments. For 10 years, he was a senior policy fellow at CGPA. In 1997, he won the prestigious Brizius Award for his contribution to public policy in governors' offices across the country. For the past two summers, he worked as a senior fellow conducting policy analysis for the Congressional Research Service at the Library of Congress.

Printed in the United States
48879LVS00002B/9